The Shapra Indians of Peru have been headhunters for several generations. Consumed with hatred against their enemies, they spear, kill, cut off heads, and set fire to houses.

Lorrie Doris Anderson and Doris Cox of the Wycliffe Bible Translators first arrive at Chief Tariri's jungle kingdom in 1950. The Shapras, puzzled by their sudden appearance, tolerate the two women, who they think are "probably looking for husbands."

TARIRI:

My Story

TARIRI:

My Story

From Jungle Killer

to Christian Missionary

as told to

Ethel Emily Wallis

HARPER & ROW, PUBLISHERS

New York, Evanston, and London

FIRST EDITION

LIBRARY OF CONGRESS CATALOG CARD NUMBER: 65-15394

D-P

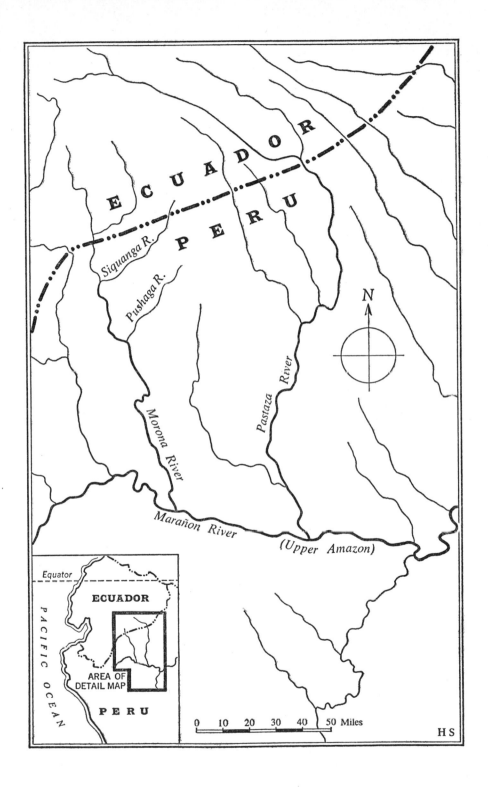

ECUADOR

PERU

Siquanga R.

Pushaga R.

Pastaza River

Morona River

Marañon River

(Upper Amazon)

N

Equator

ECUADOR

PACIFIC OCEAN

AREA OF
DETAIL MAP

PERU

0   10   20   30   40   50 Miles

H S

Contents

NOTE TO THE READER

Supplementary material to Tariri's
story appears in italic type

Autobiography?

How could a jungle Indian chief, an old hand with blow-guns but new with books, "write" his autobiography? The answer lies with those commonplace miracles of modern communication, the tape recorder and the typewriter. Unable to converse directly with Tariri in his language, I devised a series of provocative questions, such as the following, based on the story of his amazing life as I had heard it:

"What did your grandfather believe about the boa?"

"What did your father tell you about his raids on neighboring tribes?"

"How did you learn to 'take heads'?"

Tariri's answers to these questions were recorded by a team of the Wycliffe Bible Translators under whose auspices missionary work had proceeded in Tariri's tribe since 1950. John Tuggy, speaking the Shapra dialect of the Candoshi language, asked Tariri the questions. The answers were translated into English by Lorrie Doris Anderson. The tape-recorded material provided the basis on which to structure practically all of this story.

We have sought to preserve Tariri's verbal vigor by minimal editing of the original text; we have let Tariri speak for himself. This version is, of course, shorn of a great linguistic charm, Tariri's animated intonation and his inimitable imitations of jungle sounds.

My role as co-author was to direct, offstage, a dramatic monologue. It was simply the task of giving logical and literate shape to the eloquent narration invisibly written on the compact coils of magnetic tape.

Doris Cox, who with Lorrie Anderson pioneered in Tariri's tribe, is at work on a companion volume. It will complete the story by showing the other side of the coin: how two women translated the Book that changed Tariri's life.

Wycliffe member Olga Warner cheerfully executed a complex chore: the typing of the full English text translated from Candoshi, as well as the typing of the manuscript.

Eleanor Jordan of Harper & Row, a skillful detective of stumbling stones in the English reader's road, removed many of them. I deeply appreciate her interest in the project, as well as her creative help on the manuscript.

Finally, to Lucia Withers of Harper & Row, who coordinated the widespread work of the team, I would express special appreciation.

I am sure that Tariri would join me in thanking the team that helped to tell his story.

ETHEL EMILY WALLIS

TARIRI:

My Story

I

I Chant to the Boa

A shrill cry of death pierced the Peruvian jungle. It came from far out in the forest, yet the words of the wail were distinct and clear:

"My child! Oh, my child!"

They were rhythmically chanted over and over, echoing the mounting hopelessness of these who for generations had sat in darkness and in the shadow of death.

Another human cry cut through the massive dark forest. Howler monkeys answered in weird wailing calls. An owl hooted mournfully as other night birds joined the jungle chorus. Big frogs croaked, hoarse and strident.

Both cries came from Tariri's clearing where the flames from a log fire danced crazily, casting grotesque shadows against the palm thatch of a hut. Beside the fire on a crude platform of split bamboo poles an Indian mother held a dying child in her lap.

"Will you chant for my child?" the woman had asked Tariri desperately. "You have power over the boa. The child's spirit is fast going down in the water, down in the fist of the boa."

Tariri lifted his powerful voice and chanted a challenge to the boa,

"Vachisar tiavi . . . You live deep down in the water . . ."

As the blood-chilling cry rang through the forest, he fixed his gaze on the limp, dying boy before him. The woman stared stupefied at the chanter, her long black disheveled hair *falling over the child's emaciated body. In the dim light the bones seemed to protrude through the skin drawn tightly over the form of the small boy.*

Five times he saw the chonta palm blossom, and now he is dying, dying, thought the mother, numbed by sorrow and hypnotized by Tariri's cry to the boa.

"Mangoa imastang chasii . . . You have taken this child's spirit . . ."

On and on through the night the chant rose and fell on the dismal darkness as monkeys screeched and scolded in the trees towering above the hut. Tariri reached into a smoke-blackened gourd for another pinch of tobacco. He sat erect and alert, his long hair held by a crown of toucan feathers. His keen dark eyes, illumined by the firelight, were focused on the child.

Tariri would not forget the words . . . this was power . . . this was power . . . the boa would release the spirit of the child . . .

The sinister strains of the song to the boa lifted and then settled on the swampy shallows of the stream, the slimy birth-place of the mighty Amazon.

And hope was born again in the heart of an Indian mother, a heart haunted by death upon death, the dying of many children.

Look! The child has stirred!

The chant ended, and Tariri poured tobacco mixed with water between the child's parched lips. Now they would see. If the chanting had been good, with nothing left out, the child would recover. The mother watched anxiously. Tariri and the men talked in low tones, never taking their eyes from the child.

The long night hours passed silently, except for the concert of birds and beasts in the high branches of the dark forest. As the fire died away, Tariri lifted another log and lay the end of

it in the dying embers, stooping down and blowing vigor-
ously to revive the flame. A cloud of smoke and ashes filled
the dark hut and a sudden explosion of sparks drove back the
shadows—but only for a moment; the gloom returned.

The child stirred again.

Perhaps now he would live . . . Tariri had power, for he
knew the chant well . . . Perhaps the boa would release the
spirit . . .

I used to chant thus to the boa when a child became ill. Now
listen to the words:

> *Vachisar tiavi. . . .*
> You live deep down in the water,
> Down in the darkness;
> You like leaves and logs decaying
> And dwell in debris caught fast in the tree roots,
> Down under the water:
> To you I sing.
>
> *Xanaxanav tiavi,*
>   *Mpiyam tiavi,*
>   *Xanaxanav tiavi . . .*
> You love the darkness of your water home,
> But sometimes you seek the sunlight.
> Then you crawl up out of the water
> And curl up in the sunshine
> To dry yourself on the soft bank.
> As you lie there, black and shiny,
> The little bees light on your leathery hide
> And lick you.
>
> *Knana knana tiavi,*
>   *Pama pama tiavi . . .*
> You love living in the water,
> But we see you on land when the water is high

And the bank is flooded.
When the water is high
And the frogs begin to croak,
Then you come to the surface.

Pintaranga tiavi,
　　Kriri tiavi,
　　　Xoririri tiavi,
　　　　Simata tiavi . . .
Your black soft skin lies limply folded
And shines in the sunlight.
The skin on your back is shiny and soft,
Not hard like the trunk of a tree.
You just loll in the sunshine,
All limp and lazy,
And your backbone is not broad.

Kamanchaya tiavi, pontsopontso tiavi,
　　Tangarxina tiavi,
　　　Xoririri tiavi . . .
You also like the roots of the thorn palm,
And there you sometimes live
At the edge of the lake
Where the thorn palm grows,
Thick groves of thorn palms crowding the lakeside.

Mangoa imastang chasii,
　　Mangoa imastang chasii,
Novantatam mangoa isichig chasii,
　　Novantatam mangoa isichig chasii . . .
You dweller in darkness,
You have taken this child's spirit,
His spirit you have stolen to hide down deep
In the watery darkness where you dwell.
But now I defy you!
I now bring back the spirit of the sick one!

That is what we chanted when a child sick with malaria was brought to us. We did not chant just for the sake of chanting. Sometimes the child would be laid in front of three seated persons. Then we would all chant to the boa. All three would have some tobacco while the sick person lay limp. Looking at him, we would chant. We did not all chant together; one would chant by himself, and another by himself.

Thus we believed in the boa. But we had to have tobacco. We would overcome the boa when we chanted and used tobacco. The boa had caused the sickness so we had to overcome it. We believed in this for the sake of curing that illness, and they were cured. Even those that were ill far away would come to us. We were just like doctors, curing them and sending them back home.

In those days people would get sick and say, "Come, let us go and try it out again." They would even come by night. They would bring a woman. Having arrived, she would lie without moving. Or if it were a child, it would be the same. They would then leave happily.

People used to get sick and cough with pneumonia. They would complain of the pain. For that we would chant with a bit of tobacco. Crying with pain, they would drink the tobacco. After that they would stop crying and faint. They would not know anything for three days, then they might be well.

Our ancestors always said, "This made me well." This, we thought, was power. "We will always chant," we said.

We believed in the boa, the witchdoctor, the war spirit, and chanting. We really believed in this. We really loved the devil.

II

What I Learned from My Ancestors

The Candoshi trust in the boa for *arotama*, the power of long life. If a man has a certain kind of dream, he knows that the next day he will see a boa which will talk to him. When he sees the boa, he hits it with a stick. At first, it fights back and wants to kill him, but he gets a heavy vine and ties it around the boa and drags it to a cleared spot in the forest. He puts palm leaves and vines around it and makes a roof of palm leaves over it so it will not get away. Then the man sleeps nearby and dreams. In his dream the boa in the form of a man comes and gives him something shiny to swallow. This gives him *arotama*. When he wakes up, he is angry and goes and kills his enemy and has power over him.

Our ancestors said that the boa does not die, so that is why it has the power of *arotama*. "A boa just goes on living and living," they said. "A boa cannot die. So if you dream with a boa, you will live the way it does."

The jaguar spirit also gives *arotama*. The boa spirit and the jaguar spirit are the most powerful of the spirits.

Another that has the power of long life is the hawk. It kills things with its claws. It is very strong. If you grab it, it grabs you very hard, and wants to kill you. You chop off a long stick and hold the hawk down to the ground with the stick. If you have a blowgun, you may hold the hawk down with that. That is what our ancestors told us to do. They would tie it to the stick or the blowgun, and carry it on their backs. They would say, "I will make a little shelter for this bird." So they would do so and put the hawk in it for the night.

The one who has made the shelter returns home at noon the next day. The animals that he has hunted, that he has killed for his child, he takes home and throws down to his wife. Then he does not sleep with his wife. He goes back out into the woods.

"I am going to drink tobacco," he says, "so I will just drink a little bit of *masato*."

In the woods he lies near the shelter that he has made for the hawk. He lies there hungry, not eating.

He mixes fruit from the *kontoma* tree with water, and sets it aside. He lies there, resting, and mixes the tobacco drink, and drinks it at sundown. Then he chants, and as soon as he gets drunk from the tobacco, he goes to sleep.

In a dream the hawk talks to the man, just as I am talking to you. It says, "Break my arm. Do not keep your hand from me. If you keep it from me, you will die."

In the dream the man says, "Let me have your hand," and he grabs the hawk. "What an arm you have! That is a chief's arm, it is! I am going to become equal with you. I am going to come to know also. I am going to learn."

In the dream the man cannot bend his arm and the hawk says, "You will not die. You will go on living."

So he talks like that, having slept. When the moon gets to mid-sky, he unties the hawk and lets it go, saying, "That is all. I do not want to sleep in the woods any more. I will go to my house and drink *masato* and stay up the rest of the night. Something else will enter me."

Jaguars can also give *arotama*. A man comes along the path and there is a jaguar, just sitting there looking and looking. Do not be afraid. It is there for a purpose. It is there to test to see what you will do. If the ancestors saw a jaguar like that, they would poke it with a stick or a blowgun and say, "Speak to me. Who are you? You are probably a spirit. You are probably one of the ancients. What is your name? Are you Totarika, or Maama, or Korima?

Speak to me. You are probably a spirit. Otherwise, why are you just sitting there in the path?" Then they would name the names of other great ones who had died. And they would keep poking the jaguar to find out who was returned in the form of a jaguar.

The jaguar would begin to run, and would try to grab at the person, just to test him. If you are afraid, that is bad. That is what our ancestors said. If you are afraid, you will die. The jaguar will say that you are afraid. So the ancestors in talking to us would say, "Do not be afraid, be strong."

If you see a jaguar and talk to it, then you will kill someone. The jaguar does not lie. It does not talk to you for nothing. It talks about killing people, in order for you to kill people. So if it knows you and you get the power, it will be easy to kill people. That is why we are not afraid of jaguars.

The ancestors also said that the possum is without death, and is unable to die. You take a stick and beat a possum, throw the possum away and leave it there, and it comes back to life.

I cannot help laughing at the possums! We kill lots of them here. The dogs bite them, bite them all over, and go away and leave them for dead. And the next morning they are gone! That is why the ancestors said that the possum is without death.

It is said that the possum made a mess of things long ago. It married somebody's wife, and just made things bad. God got angry and went back to the sky. That is why we hate the possum.

They said that the possum has something which is shiny. It sparkles and sparkles. They said that if you take this, you will have many children, and you will live many years like the possum. The ancestors would tell us about these things and say, "Do not leave these things. Keep thinking about them."

That is what I did when I was a little boy. I would say to the other boys, "I am going out to the *chacra* and dream about a possum."

So we would go out to the *chacra* and lie down near a banana tree, and near a papaya tree, and there we would sleep. We would just lie there waiting for a possum. When the possum would climb up the tree for a papaya, it would throw it down where we were sleeping.

We would say, "The possum will speak to us. Look out! A papaya might fall on our heads and kill us!"

We were without any sense in those days.

The ancestors also told us that we could get power from certain birds. When one of those birds came near, they would grab it and put it under a clay pot. Then they would sleep near it. The Achuales said that if you do this, you get power which will cause you to take heads.

How many, many things did the ancestors talk about! They would gather together and make a big noise about it. The old folks talked, and everybody listened, especially the children. The children would say, "That is what I might do someday." Children enjoy listening to the things that the adults tell about. Look at all these that sit here, all ears, listening to us! Well, it was the same way long ago.

Our ancestors chanted for healing and for hunting. They taught us how to chant. While a person is learning to chant he fasts for a long time. For the first three days he eats nothing, not even drinking *masato*. On the fourth day he can make some thick *masato* and mix some tobacco juice with it and drink it. On the fifth day he can drink a little bit of *masato*, and for the next ten days he eats very tiny birds, and a little bit of *masato*. Forever after that he will not eat pineapple and sweet things like sugar cane and papaya. Also, he is not supposed to eat salt. A man gets very skinny, of course.

The ancestors taught us how to get lots of birds and animals. "Do not die a no-hunter," they said. "You will be a no-hunter all your life if you do not go through this tobacco chant. What woman would want you if you were a no-hunter? The women would just say, 'Oh, he is a no-hunter.' "

So the ancestors would make a shelter of palm leaves, and an old man would be in there, and the young men would enter in and sit very quietly.

The palm leaf hides the men, and the women cannot come and look at them. That is forbidden. If a woman should come and look while they are sitting in the shelter, they would become no-hunters.

I once entered a palm shelter. One of the old men taught me. I slept there for ten days, and then I went back to my house. The old man warned me not to drink strong drink because if I threw up I would lose all the power and become a no-hunter. He said, "Come on, let us go hunting. You will get lots of birds and animals real easy." So he took me out hunting.

When we got back to the house with what we had caught the older men would feed everyone. Then they would chant over the game, and blow on it, and feed the people.

Then they would tell the women to save all the bones of the animals. Poor women. They suffered, having to fuss with all those bones. One by one they would keep them, and when they got a whole bunch they would go and throw them in the water. The old men said, "That is the way you do it. If you do that, how many birds and animals you will catch!"

Another teaching was about the cutter ants. When you see the road of the cutter ants as they cut down the grass, you spit on it. You just keep spitting and spitting, whenever you see their road. That is for not forgetting. Look at the cutter ant. It does not forget. Even though it has a very little heart, it does not forget where its path is and say, "Now let us see, where was that?" And it does not get lost and say, "Now where was my path?"

It goes far from its house, far off on the path, and climbs away up high, almost up to the sky on a palm tree, and there where it sees a nice tender little leaf, it cuts it and then it climbs down again. It goes back to its house, takes the leaf inside, and feeds its babies. The cutter ant cannot forget.

So you get from it the power for not forgetting. When you have chanted to it, then you spit on the cutter ant's path. If you do that, you will not forget things. The cutter ant will tell you. It will say, "Do this, do that."

That is what the ancestors told us. Day after day they taught us these things. "Do this, do that," they said.

Our ancestors taught us not to eat deer and tapir. It is because of the children. Even if only the parents ate deer or tapir, it would make the children pale, and also they would not learn to walk as soon.

The ancestors chanted if they killed a tapir. Killing a tapir was bad if you had a baby. It caused the baby to be sick. Then they would chant for the baby to get better. The blood would show in his face again, and he would have red cheeks. They would chant and chant for many days.

Long ago our ancestors lived at the headwaters of the rivers, far away at the end of nowhere. They lived on the Yonkantari and the Manchonka. At the headwaters of the Pushaga Old Maama lived. That was his place. We just used to follow the sayings of the old ones, Maama and Mpona.

The Achuales of the Makiya River were always making war with Old Maama. The Achuales always started it. Only after that did the Candoshi kill the Achuales, only then did they go on raids through the jungle. The Achuales would come back after them. And so everybody would go out to kill. Whenever Old Maama's people killed many Achuales, they would come home and drink *masato*. They had a good time laughing together and whistling *e-e-e, o-o-o, e-e-e!* That is the way it was. They went on killing each other back and forth.

That is what my grandfather Totarika did.

There were lots and lots of people in those days, and sometimes there was not enough meat. Sometimes they would see lots of wild boar. The men would gather together and spear them. The spears were made of very hard palmwood.

My grandfather Totarika lived in a small *chacra*. Our ancestors did not have machetes to make large *chacras* with. They would use stone for axes. They would fasten the stone onto a palmwood stick and with that they would chop down the trees. Whole bunches of people would get together and chop, but they would make only a small *chacra*. The woods almost killed them. It was hard work and they were worn out. After cutting it all down, they would burn the brush and have a *chacra*.

They also used arrows for killing the wild boar. They made the bow with hard palmwood and then put a palm-fiber string on it. With that they would shoot the wild boar with the arrows, and the wild boar would be very angry and would make loud noises.

They would take them home and have a big feast. Or sometimes they would smoke the wild boar right on the spot where they speared them. They would go and get their wives and bring them back there to smoke the meat on the fire the same night. The women would paint their husbands' faces with *achiote*. They all would have a big feast in the woods. The men chopped down trees and laid them on the ground for the women to sit on. They enjoyed looking at their wives there, they said.

That is the way it was before we had blowguns. Then after awhile the ancestors were able to get machetes and were able to make shields and blowguns. They had visited some Achuales who were friendly, and they saw that they had machetes which they got through trading. They made friends with the Achuales and exchanged gifts. So they were able to get the machetes with which to make blowguns. Old Maama and Korima learned how, and taught the others. It was the Achuales who taught us how to make blowguns. That is what my father Nochumata told me. With a blowgun you can kill many monkeys or birds. They just fall silently. You can kill one after the other in the same group of monkeys or birds.

Our ancestors also trapped in order to get birds and animals. They made traps with palm-fiber string. Sometimes turtles and wild turkeys would get caught in the trap. At times even snakes, like bushmasters, would get caught. The ancestors would just kill them and throw them away.

Our ancestors fished with poison in small streams and little ponds. They got the poison from plants and vines. The best kind made the fish very drunk and easy to catch. Another kind made the fish's eyes burn and then they caught them. They hit the fish with sticks, or machetes if they had them, or they scooped them up in baskets. They did not have nets then. A whole lot of people would go at once and they had a gay time catching the fish.

They would also catch fish by weaving palm mats and putting them across the stream. It made a dam so the water upstream would be deeper than downstream. Even if the fish got through the dam, they would fall into the part where the water was very low and could be caught easily.

My grandfather Totarika lived in a swampy place among the palms. He and the other ancestors bathed in a hole made where a tree had been uprooted and later filled by rain water. My grandfather would just take a dip in the water and come up without really having bathed. One time his wife came along and said, "Why do you not really bathe?" And he said, "Why do you not marry a man who paints his face in spots with *achiote* and bathes real well?" She was afraid because he was talking bad. She probably thought, If I talk back to him or if I laugh at what he says, he will probably spear me to death. So she did not say any more and just followed him back home.

The ancestors dipped water out of the place where they bathed, and there were lots of wigglers in it. But they would heat the water until the wigglers died before they would drink it.

My grandfather did not have a good heart. He was a little bit of a devil. Maybe he was lying, but one day he said he was going to visit the monkeys where he had a wife among them. As he went along he played his little stringed instrument which said, *kang-kang, kang-kang, kang-kang,* and then his children followed him to see if he were lying.

When their father saw that they were following, he scolded them and said, "I am going by myself. Do not follow me."

But people could hear the sound of many gathered together, laughing and enjoying themselves. How could Totarika have made all that noise by himself?

Then my grandmother Tspako decided to go to see what was

going on. She saw a clearing like a big *chacra*. My father saw it, too. He said there were spider monkeys and choro monkeys and howler monkeys. Among all those monkeys there were people living. My father said that monkeys were once people. He saw lots of people dancing there. My grandmother saw the people and the monkeys, too, there in the big clearing. She told me all these things well.

Our ancestors told us that long ago in the beginning there was a big flood and there was fire at the same time. Some people became alligators and others became black panthers. In the middle of the flood a tree was standing. God lifted one child up on top of the tree during the flood. The water kept coming up and up and there the child sat on the very top of this big tree.

The child lived on the fruit of the tree. When the tree bore fruit he just picked it and ate it, and threw the seeds down in the water. At first there was just a big splash. Finally one day they just went *plunk* on the ground, and he knew that the water was down.

He climbed down from the tree and said, "I guess people used to live here." So he wandered all around but found no people, just their houses all burned down. There was nobody left, so the poor child said, "What am I going to do?" And he cried. As he was crying he said, "Well, I am going to hunt around further," and he went to another place and there was a person wandering around.

It was God, Apanchi, the name of the ancestors for the high God. They say it was God, and He was in his *chacra* eating *ají*. As the child wandered around watching the person who was eating *ají*, he heard a noise, *tote, tote, tote*. He said, "Maybe that is a person. I am going to see who it is." He saw a woodpecker. As it pecked and pecked, sparks would fly and soon a little piece of glowing wood fell down. The child took it. That was the way the Candoshi got fire.

God came to live among them for awhile. They took care of Him and He lived there. He would take feathers of birds and make other birds of them. He would go fishing in the streams also. He would go off by Himself, and after awhile He would come back with a big pile of fish. They would all be big fish, not a lot of these tiny things. He was a better fisherman than anybody else. People began to say, "Why, this must be God because He is better than everyone else!" He even caught more fish than anybody else.

Being very angry, they killed Him.

Our ancestors told us how a hummingbird took a man up to heaven. There were only two people in the world, a young man and his mother. At night they would lie outside and chat, just the two of them. The young man, lying there looking at all the beautiful stars twinkling up above, said, "Oh, Mother, if I could just have a star for my wife!"

The next night a spirit came to him and said, "When I come to you and enter into your navel and you feel something real, real cold wiggling there, do not cry out. Just be strong and quiet. Do not say anything when I come."

So the next time he was lying there with his mother out under the stars talking, the spirit came to him and entered into his navel and it was very cold. It just wiggled and wiggled there. You cannot imagine how cold it was! But he was strong and did not cry out.

A person was born from that, a woman who spoke to the young man. So there were the two of them on one bamboo platform, and the mother was over on a separate platform. The man and the woman laughed.

The mother called out, "With whom are you laughing?"

And the young man said, "I am just laughing by myself. I have no wife to laugh with." For the star wife had told him, "Do not tell your mother. Do not let her know about us at all."

The mother and the son went out hunting and the man said to his mother, when he had brought home what they caught, "Save out for me the heads and the wings and the tails."

So the mother prepared the animals and the birds, and took out these parts, and also the feet, and gave them to her son. He took them and shared them with his wife, and they laughed together.

The mother came running out and said again, "With whom are you laughing?"

The wife said, "Do not tell her about me." But by then she had two children. She said, "When I have many children, your mother will see me."

Then one time the man was whittling away at darts for his blowgun, and the wife was inside a canoe that he had made. The wife said again, "When I have many children, your mother will see me."

She was inside the canoe with her two children. The man went out hunting and the mother said, "My son did not get me any firewood. What am I going to use for my fire? Well, I am going to chop up this canoe and use it for firewood to cook my yuca." But when she began to chop, a person screamed. The mother dropped her ax in fright, and the wife went off screaming, "Your mother is splitting my head open!" And the two little children climbed out of the canoe and followed her. The mother looked on in amazement and said, "Who are these? I suppose it is my son's wife and his children." So she called, "Come back! Come back!"

But they ran fast and came to where the husband was, and he called out, "Come here!" But the wife went right on as fast as she could, and disappeared from view. He was very sad and went and raved at his mother. "What did you want to go and touch that for, Mother? Did I not tell you not to chop that?" He grabbed his spear and went chasing after his mother with it.

Then he sat down and just stayed there crying all day, and the sun went down, and he cried the next day, and the sun went down, and he did that for five days. His wife had already gone back up to the sky with her children.

After five days he heard some noise and a lot of people came along, buzzards and eagles, that sort of bird. Buzzards and eagles used to be people, you know. So they came to his house and said, "You kill your mother. If you kill your mother, then you will see your wife again. You wife is up in the sky. We will take you up where your wife is."

So the young husband, who did not have any sense, said, "All right," and he told his mother to go cut some bananas. The buzzards and other birds said, "Well, did you kill your mother?" And he said, "Yes, I killed her."

They went off to where he had killed his mother and began to gobble up her flesh until there was nothing left but bones. Then they went to the man and one of them, a kind of eagle, said, "Get on my back, and I will take you to where your wife is." So he got on the bird's back and it took off, but its wings just went flutter, flutter, flap, flap, and it could not get very far. It said to the man, "You're just too heavy."

The buzzard said, "I will try it." So the buzzard took off with the man on its back, and they went up to the top of the tallest trees, but could not go any farther. It took him back and set him down again. All of the birds tried, but they all failed.

So the man cried, "What am I going to do?" Then the buzzards and all the other birds said, "Just wait here. We can come back with your wife." And they flew off until the man could not see them.

The young man thought, I wonder where my mother's body is? He went and looked, and there was nothing left but her bones. He cried harder. "Now I will suffer even more. What is going to happen to me?" And he ran here and ran there. The poor man just could not live alone.

Then the hummingbird came. Out on the path the man heard a shrill little whistle, *shoon, shoon, shoon.* "Who is that?" he said. "Who are you, brother?" the hummingbird called. Then the man said, "I killed my mother. The buzzard told me to, so I killed her." The hummingbird said, "No, you should not have done that. Why did you kill her by yourself? You cannot go to see your wife alone. If I am not here, you cannot go to see her." "How do you think I could get up there?" said the man. "I can take you up," replied the hummingbird. "I saw your wife. She is up in the sky."

So the man said, "All right," and the hummingbird took him on its back, and off they went.

Our ancestors said that the sky is open, at the top there is an opening, and it keeps opening and closing, opening and closing, and it keeps going *dee-at, dee-at, dee-at,* trying to kill anyone who tries to get through. The hummingbird just stood there in front of it, beating its wings without stopping, and standing in the same place.

It was trying to get through. It kept fluttering and fluttering, and after awhile it said, "I am getting tired." So then the opening opened a little bit again, and dash! it went right through and they were in!

They found themselves in a *chacra*. When the hummingbird had set him down, it gave the man a stick and said, "Your wife is over there digging yuca. When she goes to put her basketful of yuca on her back, you point this at her. She will be in a line with her sister, digging, but you point this at her, and the bark strap of her basket will break. She will fix it, and put it on her head again. You point this at her and it will happen again. Just keep doing that, and you can catch her. When she asks you who brought you here, you tell her that you came all by yourself."

So the man sat there facing the women digging yuca, and when their baskets were heavy, he pointed at them and his wife's basket strap broke, and the basket fell down. She said to her sister, "Wait a minute," and she tied it together and put it on her head again. She went a little farther and it broke again. Her sister said, "I am getting tired. I will go on ahead and rest at the house and you come when you are ready."

So while his wife was trying to tie her basket up again, the young man went and threw his arms around her.

The wife said, "Where are you going? Who is this?"

The young man said, "I just climbed up here all by myself." She said, "How could you climb up by yourself? Some person must have brought you. My father will kill you. He has gone off to kill some people. His name is Thunder. I will get some of my father's *piripiri* to rub on you." So she rubbed him all over with *piripiri*.

Her father, Thunder, returned. "Baah! Baah!" thundered the father Thunder. "Hmmmm, what person around here has been rubbing on lots of my *piripiri*? Hmmmm, what kind of person? Who has come here? Who, who, who, who, who?" And he sounded very fierce, and everyone was afraid.

He took stones and threw them where the young man was, but he did not kill him. The man just kept popping up. So Thunder said, "Why is he like that?" Thunder threw fire on him. He kept throwing fire, and throwing fire, but nothing happened.

Finally Thunder said, "He must have a heart like mine. I cannot get the best of him." Then he said to the young man, "All right, talk to me and I will listen." As the person talked, Thunder crackled and crackled, and the woods caught on fire. The lightning flashed around the woods, and it lit up.

That is what our ancestors said about the man who climbed up to the sky. But maybe they were talking about God.

III

My Father Was a Killer

My grandfather Totarika was a terrible killer. He killed and killed. My father Nochumata went killing with his father. He followed his father and was taught by him. Old Maama and Korima also taught my father how to kill. They each had their own hard palmwood spear when they went out to kill.

There were many, many Candoshi away back then. Now they are almost all gone. Our ancestors lived around Lake Rimachi and on all those rivers there. Now the people have gone to many other places. They ran away. All the big chiefs and the older ones were killed and only the young men were left over. The people ran away so they would not be killed by their enemies.

My father lived on the Chuinta River. How many people there were then! He was the chief of the Shapra people of the Candoshi. There were many other chiefs also. Each one lived in his own place and had his own people.

Most of the Candoshi were killed by the poison darts of the Achuales. Sometimes they would shoot the darts one after another and they would shoot Candoshi in the nose. If the man could get quickly to where there was water and drink lots and lots of water, he might get well, but if there was no water for a long time, he would die. If the poison made him dizzy, he would be almost out of his head and would run wildly through the woods. Even if he could not find a stream, if he could find a palm tree which has a canoe-shaped leaf that falls down, there would be rain water caught in it and he could drink it and that would help.

The Achuales also killed many of our people with spears.

My father Nochumata was very great and very strong. How many people he killed! He went killing with his friend Chumpi. They killed Huambisas and Achuales. My father would gather together many men from the Chapuri and the Chuinta rivers. They did whatever he ordered. They killed many Achuales on the Mawuia River. But my father did not make war with the men of his own tribe. "Why should we make war with the Candoshi?" he said. "They are our own flesh and blood." With the other Candoshi chiefs he had talking parties, and then they would go and kill.

"Be strong, and do not be afraid," my father told me. "If you are like that, you will be a great chief and you will be greater than all the others."

Our ancestors taught us, "If people come to your house to make an attack, do not be afraid. You just chase them back into the woods and kill them. If you do not, they will kill you."

When boys are about ten years of age, they are told, "Spend time with the *koraka*, the chief. Spend time with the *korakas*, the people who kill."

The men had two spears made of hard palmwood. They would spear somebody with one, and then spear somebody with the other, and they would quickly teach the young ones what to do. If the person who had been speared was still alive, the young boys learned to kill by spearing him. That is how they would get over their fear of killing.

My father taught me by word of mouth, then I went out with the men to kill. How many times I went along to be taught, to learn! At first you just go. You do not kill somebody right off. You have to go for a long time with the *korakas* to learn how it is done. But you do not just stand there idle. After someone has speared a person and he is screaming, "Yay! Yay!" you spear that one.

At first a person cannot kill very well and he says, "Oh, what will I do? How will I do it?" One of the *korakas* would say, "You cannot kill right off. Do not try it yet. You young ones have no sense. You might spear someone who has a gun in his hand and he will shoot you. Do not go off on your own. Follow right after me. Do not leave me. You follow me, and when I kill somebody, when he is just dying, you spear him. Spear him so that he will die quickly."

I was very young when my father died. A witchdoctor cursed him and he died. That is what they say. I was there when he died. He took my hand as he was dying and said lots of things to me. "I am dying," he said. "You stay. You do this and that. You look after your mother and look after your sisters. You have many sisters. Look after them."

They killed a lot after my father died. I went many times with the *korakas*. We would come back to sleep a few days in the house, then we would go again. We would sleep a few more days, and again we would go. We went on one raid after another.

We young ones would say, "Look, we are tired. We have carried all these heavy bananas, yuca, and other things. Let us rest." So we would rest ten days at the house and then they would say, "Let us go," and we would be off again.

Before leaving, we would call all the people together. The houses were very big and they would be filled with people. They would chant and say, "We are going to go and kill." There would be many of them making lots of noise. You could hear them all over.

There would be some young men who did not want to go. They were afraid and wanted to stay at home. "I had a bad dream," they said. "I had a bad dream and that means that someone will kill me." The older ones would scold the young ones and say, "How is it that you do not have a heart like mine? Look, your father is a great killer. Why do you want to be a no-killer, and just sit around the house?" So the young ones would think about it and come to their senses and say, "All right."

They ate lots of *mota* root. "You look on," the older men said to the younger ones. We could not touch it. "That is the way you do it," they said. "Someday you can do the same. If you eat the *mota*, you will not die. After the *mota* dies, it grows again." That is what the old ones did and that is what they believed, and we looked on. All of us sat there on the platforms and saw them eat the *mota*. That is the way you teach your children.

So I said to myself, That is what I will do someday. I kept thinking about that, and that is what I kept in my heart. That is the very thing I believed and thought, and I said, Someday when I have children I will teach them also.

The first thing my father taught me was about witchdoctors, and that is what I thought about. And I said, "When I grow up I will be a witchdoctor. Then I will blow on people, and they will love me very much. They will pay me. They will give me things to help me. That is the way they do it. They give people tobacco and other things to drink."

My father told me about his brother Warispa who was a witchdoctor. He said, "Look at all the things he gets. He gets toucan feathers. He gets skirts and machetes. Whatever he wants, people give him for the medicine that he gives them." And I thought, I would like to get those things, too. I will be like him.

I was little, but growing, and was just beginning to lose my teeth when my father told me about these things. I talked with my uncle Warispa. He said to me, "There are white things, magic darts, with which you will be able to heal a sick person. There are also the slippery things which you cough up when you are healing well. Then you will make the sick people better. If you do that, people will love you. Look at all the people who love me! Look at how many people keep coming here for me!

"When you grow up I will give you the power, but you must learn first, you must grow up in your thinking. Be like me."

And I remember that well. It was a long time ago, but I remember it. My uncle blew on the *masato*. He chanted as he blew. My father told him, "Now do it for this one. I want my child to grow up with that power. When he gets older he can drink *ayahuasca* and become a witchdoctor."

After my uncle blew on the *masato* for me, I drank it. I was just a child, and I did not have any sense, and I laughed. My uncle was annoyed and said, "I suppose you are doing this for nothing. My children often mix things. Before you know it, they have eaten something that is taboo. If you eat the wrong thing, you will not learn. You will not ever learn to be a witchdoctor."

However, my uncle died and I never learned. After he had become sick he just ran wild. He would dash off here and dash off there and he kept saying, "Look out! Somebody is going to kill me, somebody is going to kill me!" Many times he would run away and my poor father could not sleep at night. He had to sit up all night without sleeping, day after day. Then my father said, "I will kill him! Just wait. After my brother has died I will go after the one who has cursed him and will kill him."

Then my father said to me, "If I should die while I am out killing, remember my words. Do not throw away my words. Keep those words in your heart."

After my uncle died my father said, "If you think of the devil and say, 'I want to learn to become a witchdoctor,' with whom will you train? Your uncle is dead. You had better forget it." Then very quickly after my uncle's death my father went to kill. He killed the witchdoctor Tsirimpo in revenge for my uncle's death.

It was soon afterward that my father died.

IV

We Learn to Take Heads

My uncle Kasimoro and his friend named Mbisa taught me, and I went out with them to kill. They even taught me how to take heads. "Do it this way," they said.

But it was the Achuales who really taught our people how to take heads. We did not take heads before that. We just speared people and left them lying. Then the ancestors said, "Well, I guess they just cut the head here, and cut it there." Then they cut the heads off. They put a small cord through the hole in the man's ear lobes and dragged it to the place where they were going to sleep. Then they would cut the hair off. They would take little bunches of hair about the size of a woman's small finger and stick them together with beeswax and lay them aside, one by one. They made beautiful headdresses of them, with toucan feathers. People would tie their hair back with them and they would hang down their back. That is what our ancestors did. They would wear their hair that way for awhile. When they killed somebody else, they would get his hair and make another headdress.

Our ancestors went to some friends who were Achuales and asked them what was a good way to take heads. "How do you do it when you kill?" they asked them. Then Chumpi, who is now dead, and my namesake Tariri, who was also a chief, went to the Achuales to learn how to take heads well.

"How do you take heads?" those Achuales asked them.

"This is the way we do it," they said. "We just cut it off and chop the hair off. We do this when we take the head with us where we sleep."

"No! That is not the way to do it!" the Achuales said. "That is no good. That is an ugly way to do it. You must cut it down lower, all nice and neat. You do not just chop it off halfway down the neck. You cut it down by the collarbone so that it can be sewed up neatly. Then after you have done that, you cure it."

"I want to see it done for myself," said my namesake. So he and his friend went with the Achuales, and together they killed. "How will he do it?" he said. "Now I will see how they shrink someone's head."

They grabbed the head and cut it down low. "Be careful," the Achuales said. The bone of the vertebra popped and it went *kwah*. Then they took the head and said, "Where shall we sleep tonight? Come on! Let us go! After killing someone you run away, you run real fast. Come on! Let us go! Oh-oh-oh-oh, look out! They might come after us. Look out! They might meet us along the way, they might catch up with us. Do not be afraid! Be strong, be strong! Stand firm!"

When it grew dark they stopped and slept some place, and made camp. While they had someone working on a head, they had others hiding in the bushes to watch out for the enemy. "They might come," they said. "You stay here and watch, and we will shrink the head."

"How is it done?" my namesake asked.

And the Achuales said, "You do it this way. You blow and blow, and you lay the head there. You lay the hair here like this, and then you scalp it. You do it very carefully here by the eyes as you take the skin off the skull. You cut very carefully, like this, very slowly, and be careful when the skin is very thin. Then you stop cutting. Here at the mouth you poke something through, a stick or a dart, and later you sew the mouth up. Be very careful when you cut the inside of the nose.

"After you have cut off the scalp, you cure it. Make a fire and put a small clay pot of water on it, and put the head into that. Let it boil well. At the same time put some small stones into the fire to get real hot. Into the pot also put some strands of spun cotton, in order to grab the head. Be very careful about this, for if one hair of that head falls to the ground, that would be a very bad sign. You will die very quickly. Get a good hold on the head with this cotton through the hole in the ear lobes, and take it out of the pot. Then put the stones into the head. Pick them up with sticks and drop them into the hole. They are glowing red hot and they go *chu-u-u-uh!* as they fall into the head.

"The person's hair is very long, and it comes out pretty. When the head is all cooked, then you sew it up. You sew up the back, from the crown down, where you slit it. When it is all sewed and pretty, if the sun is shining you hang it in the sun. Where the sun rises, where God made the sun, is where the head should be facing when it is put out to dry. Make the head face toward the rising sun so you will not die. When the sun goes past midday, you make the head face toward the setting sun."

That is what they did. They made the person's nose face toward the rising sun until afternoon, and then it would face toward the setting sun and his crown would have its back to the rising sun.

After many days they smell it, and if it smells all right, it is ready. They take a few stitches out at the back of the head and pour some *achiote* into the hole they have made there. That makes it smell good. Then they put a cord through it and it is hung around someone's neck.

So a man wears the head around his neck, and he calls all of his friends. He sends word to this one and that one, saying, "Come, let us drink *masato* at my house. Come visit me, brother." He paints his face with *achiote* the way our ancestors did. The faces come out pretty when the men paint themselves like that. This one and that one would get a head, and eventually everyone would have a head around his neck.

One who kills someone and takes his head and shrinks it becomes a chief. Our ancestors learned, and taught us. It was a man who killed and took many heads who became greater than all other people. He became a great chief.

But we ourselves are afraid. When we see a head hanging around someone's neck, we say, "That might happen to me someday. They might take my head like that and hang it around someone's neck." That is what we say among ourselves.

It was very sad when the head of a man's son would be taken. He would say, "My child's head is away off there some place." It was the enemy Achuales who took the heads of our young ones. Then the men would say, "Someday I will go again and get my son's head back. I will go there and bring back my child."

After a man has had a head for a long time he gets tired of it. Some relative will say to him, "Let me wear it for awhile. You have killed lots of people, and you have had lots of heads to wear." After hearing that he will give it to his relative. That is the kind of person who does not go out to kill. He is old and just stays in the house to talk and to give orders. The old people are the ones that would ask to have the heads for awhile.

In those days there were lots of heads. Many of the heads would be around for awhile and the ants would eat some of them. On others the hair would begin to fall out. "That is bad," the men would say. So they would use the hair for headdresses with feather ornaments, sometimes mixing it with toucan tail feathers for tying their hair back.

Then our ancestors went to the Huambisas. "How do they shrink heads?" they thought, and they wanted to learn from them. They made friends with a group of Huambisas and asked them what they did when bugs and ants got into the shrunken heads. The Huambisas taught them how to do it right.

But the Huambisas said, "They are no good once the bugs are in them. Then you make a belt out of the hair. You weave the hair into a belt and wear it around your waist. We cut the hair off the scalp and spin it. We weave it into a belt. It takes the hair from two heads to make it as wide as it is supposed to be. If you want it really wide, it takes the hair from three heads. To make it even wider, it takes the hair from lots of heads."

That is what the Huambisas taught us to do.

When my father went on killings, he would sometimes force people to come back with him. But he would kill the young boys. He would spear them because they would grow up to kill him in return.

After my father began to shoot with bullets, sometimes a child would be killed by mistake. But my people did not really want to kill children. When the children saw the killings, they would scream and scream, and so they would leave them alone. After a child had been killed by mistake, the next time the enemy would kill one of ours. Then our ancestors said, "Let us not kill the children. Let us be a good example by not killing children. It will be worse for us if we kill them." And so they let the children alone.

They took the women for wives. My father had six wives. But not I! I had only two. Three of my father's wives were Huambisas, and three of them were Candoshis. Women just make a fuss. Even when my father made a great big platform for his wives and their children, it was crowded and they hated among themselves. The men loved their wives, but the women fought with each other. The women would scold among themselves, then the man would scold a wife and say, "Do not do that. Do not talk like that. That is enough. What do you act like that for?" My father suffered a lot because of that. He could not even sleep sometimes. They would say, "What do you want to be with her for? Why do you neglect me?" Each wife wanted his attention.

Many of my father's children died.

I wanted to kill in order to take many women. Then I would have many wives and raise many children. We would be one big happy family, I thought. I wanted to marry at least five women because it is impossible for just one woman to have many children. One woman has one child and then much later, many moons later, she will have another. That is no good.

After I married two women I still wanted to get more. Tsirimpo's mother, Marasho, the first one, did not nag me. She just sat there quietly and did not say anything. She did not seem to care, so

I married Irina as my second wife. Then after Marasho died, Irina kept telling me all the suffering her father went through with more than one wife. "My father suffered, and my mother suffered," she said. "How many times did my mother cry! That is the way it is with women when there is more than one wife. They cannot live happily and in peace." After I thought about those things, I said, "All right, I will not marry another one. You alone I will take along. You will be the only one."

When I really learned to kill, sometimes we could not get many people to go. Once four of us went together. I killed an Aguaruna. He was a chief, a very great chief.

But I did not just go and get angry on my own and kill this man. An Aguaruna had come to me, begging me for help. He said, "Help me, friend. A man has killed my two brothers and killed my father. He killed my poor old father. Come and see. Come to my house." So I went to see, and there his father had just been shot, and there was the blood all over and it was smelly. So that was why the Aguaruna was crying. He said to me, "Why should you not help me? If I were a killer like you, I would help everybody. If you help me, I will give you a woman."

Then I said, "I don't want a woman! Wait! Do not talk about that. We do not want to think about women in this revenge killing. Let us talk about the man."

We went with some Huambisas, who were able to talk with the Aguarunas. We went far along the Cangasa River. There are lots of rivers over there. We had to climb up a mountain, very high, and then another one, and there were great big rocks and we climbed and climbed. My feet hurt.

We came to the enemy Aguaruna's house. There was a *chacra*, just like mine here, and a path leading to it. I went along the path, and the others with me came along. Then we looked in the house. There was nobody there. They had all run away. But they were close by and started shooting at us. We were strangers and they knew that we had come to kill, so they were shooting at us. We shot back, and they fell over dead, just like that. So the Aguaruna with me was very happy. "Let us go see," he said. "Here! This is the one that killed my relatives. This one right here. He is the chief!" He was so excited that he kept saying that over and over.

Then I said, "Did he take the heads of your relatives? If he did, then we will take the heads here too. Do not be afraid to tell me."

"No, he did not," the Aguaruna said. "He did not take ours."

And so we left them. We returned home. That was all we did. My heart was happy after we shot them. My heart was happy.

But the very first time I went to kill with a gun and the guns of the enemy began to explode, I was really scared. It is not the same as killing with a spear. You only go after someone who is empty-handed, somebody who is just sitting there, just kind of dreaming. You can dash at him and spear him. That way you are able to kill quickly, that is easy.

Our people kill when it is almost wanting to get dark. It is hard to follow anyone in the dark, to go after anyone when he runs away. So returning from the raids we would light beeswax flares. We would sleep far away, and then come out on the other side of the forest, far away. That is what our ancestors taught us to do. If you kill early in the morning, someone can follow after you. They can kill you out in the woods. If you kill people at noon, they can follow you and kill you. Kill people at sundown, the ancestors told us. You can run away in the dark if necessary. If you get tired, then rest. That is the way they always told us, and that is the way we did.

V

The Kirinko Come to Our River

Hidden at the haunted headwaters of the Amazon in a dense jungle area, Tariri's Shapra tribal group had only fragmentary information of life beyond their own green world. An occasional venturesome Peruvian trader was their only narrow channel of communication. Their patrón spoke Candoshi, but the Indians spoke no Spanish. The image of outsiders that was projected into the obscure corner of northern Peru as it merges into Ecuador's back door was at best a vague threat to tribal security. The image of the American, the kirinko, furnished by their patrón and compounded by tribal lore, never failed to conjure up wild and weird fantasies. Victorino was one notable exception among patróns.

I hated the white man and stood ready to kill any who might come to my domain. I was Ruler of the Seven Rivers.

Our *patrón* who lived downriver on the Pushaga told us, "Kirinko want to come and live with you."

"Why do they want to come?" we asked. We were unhappy.

"Your talk is not good," the *patrón* said. "You talk ugly all the time. If you talk like that to the *kirinko*, they will kill you."

I said, "Let them kill me. I am not afraid."

After that the *patrón* said, "You are a brave one!" He felt I was a great chief.

I thought in my heart, Why should they live with us? What

44

for? They probably want to take away our lands. I went to the *patrón* and asked him, "Do they want to take our lands?"

"I think so," he said. "That is why all the *kirinko* want to come here."

I thought in my heart, Why would they do that? The *kirinko* did not come to our ancestors. Our grandfathers Totarika and Maama told us about *inkaresa* [Englishmen]. They make guns and all kinds of things. They did not tell us about living with the *kirinko*. Why should they come and live with us now? What do they want? Now we will see.

"All of them want to come here," said the *patrón*.

I was sad when I heard that.

"You do not live well," he said. "You talk bad. When you do that they will slash you. They have long machetes. They will slit your throat from ear to ear as you stand there alive. They kill and kill. They do not allow laziness."

That is what he said, and laughed.

Well, let them do that to me. I am not afraid. Why should I be afraid? But I thought a lot about it.

Then I went away one day and when I returned my brother Tsowinki said, "They came while you were gone. Two *kirinko* came. They came to see us."

Wycliffe members Harold Goodall and David Beasley made a trip to the area with Victorino, searching out a location for the Beasleys who had thought of working with the Shapra group of the Candoshi tribe. However, the Beasleys decided to settle in the neighboring Huambisa tribe.

My relatives did not know who the two *kirinko* were. They said, "They might be Peruvians, but they have very white skin. Who are they? They are another kind of people. They are very white and they are very tall."

They visited in this house and that house, then they came to my house.

"Whose house is this?" they asked.

My brother-in-law Old Chiriapa, who was there at the time, said, "This is Tariri's house."

Then they asked, "Who here is a great talker? Who is the great talker? Who is the great one here?"

Then my brother-in-law said, "Tariri is strong here, and this is his house."

We kept wondering who the *kirinko* were that came with Victorino. How did I happen to miss them? I wish I could have seen them. What are the *kirinko* like? I want to see their faces.

After a few days Victorino came back. He was a Peruvian but he spoke some Candoshi.

"Look," he said, "some señoritas are coming. They are coming to help you."

So I said, "Well, why should any señoritas stay here? What do they want? Why should that kind of person live with us?"

"In order to teach you God's Word," he said. "That is what they will talk about."

Victorino brought lots of cloth and shirts. "This is what the señoritas sent to pay you for working for them," he said. "They hope you will build their house. When they come they will pay you more for having built their house."

We said to Victorino, "Talk to us first and tell us all about it. You tell us and we will listen."

He talked and talked and said, "The señoritas want you to do this and that, so do this and that."

We were not sure. We said, "Maybe Victorino is just saying this. Maybe it is not the truth."

Why do they want to come? Maybe after all it is God. I thought about that in my heart. Maybe they will talk about God. The ancestors had told us something about Him. "Powerful *wiracocha* will come someday," they said. Who are these very great *wiracocha* who will come? Which ones are they?

I did not know what to think.

"Let us wait and see," we said to Victorino. "Let us see what they teach us and what they say. We will try this out."

"All right," said Victorino. "Get to work and build a house."

One day in July, 1950, Lorrie Doris Anderson and Doris Cox were flown to the Morona, near Tariri's river, by Wycliffe's Jungle Aviation and River Service—JAARS personnel —in a small float plane. A larger plane carried their equipment and supplies to their house. Victorino had helped Tariri in overseeing the building of a house for the women.

Having heard tall tales about foreigners and never having seen an airplane, Tariri was baffled when he saw this half bird, half canoe, swoop down from the sky and invade his domain. He was even more mystified about the motives of the strange arrivals, including the two women who were going to live with them.

As we were there on the Pushaga, Victorino said, "There it comes! *Two* are coming!" Then two canoes came roaring overhead. But these are not canoes! I thought. They go in the sky! First we saw them, and then we lost them. They might grab us, we thought. They might grab us and put us in these things. Even though we were a little bit afraid, we went down to meet them on the Morona River.

As we came along in our canoes we looked at theirs. Our eyes nearly popped out! We had never seen things like that before. They shone white in the sunlight, two of them. We stopped paddling and our canoes drifted while we looked. It was the first time some of us saw *kirinko*. What are they like? Now we will see. They come along in canoes that go in the sky. We heard that they make everything. These are the very things they made. We wondered at their canoes, never having seen them before. We wondered at the *kirinko*, never having seen people like that before.

We saw people in the two canoes. It is probably a chief, we

thought, not knowing. Probably only a chief would have a canoe like that. Thinking that, we looked and looked.

The people climbed up the bank and stood there. As we looked, there stood sisters Monchanki and Mpawachi [Lorrie Anderson and Doris Cox]. Who are they? we thought, and stared. We had on old, ragged clothes. Theirs were new and white. We never had seen such dresses as the girls wore. Their dresses were long and they looked like *shoroshoro* birds that swish their tails as they walk to and fro. Why are they like that?

Victorino said, "Get out and help the señoritas!" We got out and stood there, still staring. That must be the way they always are, we thought. Then Mpawachi looked into my eyes and laughed. We wondered why, since we were frightened.

They grabbed our hands. Why do they do that? They might put us in the canoes. Worried like a child, I let my hand fall. All the younger ones were staring also. I was thinking many things. There was once a man who came and took people to work for him. Maybe these have the same thing in mind. I thought maybe the *kirinko* would do that. I, by myself, was thinking these things in my heart. I do not think the others were thinking this, just I.

Then they began to take the many things up the bank. Victorino told us to help. We were still afraid, but we helped. They piled up things in our house and Victorino said, "These are the things *kirinko* make."

Victorino had said, "Build them a house." We worked and worked, but before we had finished building the house, they came. What shall we do? we thought. There is nothing we can do about it. We went to meet the girls when they came. We lived upriver on the Pushaga then, near the Tamshiyaco. When we lived near the Tamshiyaco, they came. Other Candoshi came. I sent word that the *kirinko* had come. "Really?" they said. "Are you not afraid? Are they always like that?"

Even though I was a chief, I did not know what to think about them. "These are probably goddesses, for their hair is so light," we

Chief Tariri of the Shapra tribe in Peru, with painted face and toucan feather headdress worn in the early days of missionary work in his area.

Rear view of Tariri's headdress.

Daughter Antariya mixes *masato*, the basic food drink made of *yuca*.

Tariri's thatched house with raised platform, as seen from the Wycliffe Bible Translators' first location in his tribe.

A Shapra woman shapes a clay bowl by the traditional manual process of the tribe.

Young Shotka, son of Chiriapa who was killed by the upriver Shapra group, furnishes a secure perch for his jungle pet.

Happy faces of children of Tariri's group reflect freedom from fear of attacks by neighboring groups which once threatened his people.

Tariri's present house by a lake, as viewed from the translators' location. Visitors relax in the front area which has no walls or floor; in the rear, a walled area encloses sleeping space and storeroom.

Shiniki, Tariri's half-brother, teaches in the first bilingual school among the Shapra Candoshi sponsored by the Peruvian government. Tariri's son Tsirimpo (in back row wearing glasses) studies, preparatory to becoming a teacher himself.

Tariri (left) and other adults visit the bilingual school as Shiniki teaches reading.

Shiniki and his pupils outside the schoolroom.

Adults observe as pupils smile in amusement at teacher Shiniki's remarks.

Shiniki drills his pupils.

Young Yampisa prepares to recite for his teacher Shiniki.

Tariri and Lorrie Doris Anderson concentrate on preliminary Bible translation as his daughter Matarina looks on.

The three men shown with Tariri are from the upriver Shapra group. They fled from their area after the killing of Chief Shotka's sons. They lived with Tariri's group for a time. Left to right: Manto, Old Shiniki, Tanchima, Tariri.

Tariri as he appeared during his first years of association with the Wycliffe Bible Translators.

In 1955 Tariri met Peruvian officials during his first visit to Lima. He is wearing tribal ornaments made of green beetle wings and jungle seeds.

Tariri, who had just begun to learn "letters," proudly signs his name for Cameron Townsend, Director of the Wycliffe Bible Translators.

The chief and his family at Jungle Base Yarinacocha about 1957. Back row: Mayanchi, Irina holding baby Arosa, Tariri, Tsirimpo; front row: Antariya, Matarina, Totarika, Oroshpa.

said to one another. When we asked Victorino, "Are these goddesses?" he said, "No, they are señoritas. They are *kirinko*. They
are the people who make guns and cloth and everything."

We thought of running away. We talked among ourselves. I
asked Victorino, "What is this all about? Tell us. You speak Candoshi."

"They came to tell you good news," he said, "but you will have
to teach them your language. When they have learned Candoshi,
then they will tell you. It is about God. All of you listen. Help the
señoritas well. Teach them, work for them. Do not be unwilling. If
you help them, they will give you things. They have lots of medicine and with that they will heal you. They will stab you with
it."

"Stab? Will they stab us with spears? How will they stab us?"

"With a little sharp needle they will stab and the medicine will
enter you. With that you will get well. You will not die any
more."

So we talked much with Victorino.

The Peruvians had told us, "They give another kind of medicine. The *kirinko* have a medicine that can cause everyone to die.
No one would be left."

At first we did not want to eat their food. We were afraid they
would give us poison. We did not want their medicine at first,
either. We were afraid it was poison. Why should we take it? Let
them drink their own medicine! Our ancestors did not drink this to
get well.

The men who brought the girls said, "We brought the señoritas
here. Look after them, look after them well." So I said, "All right,
I'll look after them."

But we were puzzled.

Old Shotka, the upriver chief, said to me, "Why are the *kirinko*
here? No doubt to kill. Why did they come to live with you? No
doubt they want to kill you. You will be the first one to be killed."

Later the women learned from the Shapras that they thought women were sent first, and then foreign men would come to kill. "Old Shotka wanted to kill you," they said. "If you had been men, he would have killed you. Look at the Aucas. They killed the five men who came to them."

VI

The Kirinko Learn Our Language

When the girls came they did not know our language. They could not say the words right. Poor girls! They could not get along very well. Because they were like that I was very sad.

I thought to myself, Why did they send us this kind of people? They seem stupid. Why did they send us people who cannot talk? They would try to talk and their mouths would open and close, open and close, and nothing would come out. They are pitiful, trying to say our words. Our sisters, Monchanki and Mpawachi, wanted to know our words but they were not able to talk.

I wanted very much to teach them, and so sitting there I would teach them. I wish I could teach them our language fast, I thought. They arrived from far away, even leaving behind their mothers and fathers and grandfathers, and suffered among us. How could you learn someone else's language with different words fast in a few days? It is hard to learn someone else's language, so they suffered and got thin. I saw it for myself.

They would often look at a book for many days. Then they would talk. We wondered why they would always bow their heads, close their eyes, and talk. "What do they do that for?" we said. When they knew a little of our language, they said, "We are talking about God's Word, and we also talk with God."

So I said, "What do you do that for? What good is God's Word, anyway?"

They said, "God has great power over us. He is the only one who really loves. That is the way God is. That is why we want to learn your language. We want to teach all of you in your language of what God says."

In the beginning they told us about trees. "God planted the trees," they said.

"What do you mean by saying they were planted?" we wanted to know.

"God planted them," they said. That was one of the first things they taught us.

But poor things, they would say, "What do you call this?"

"A tree."

"What is it doing?"

"Standing."

Then they would dig and say, "What do you call it when you do this?"

"Planting."

"Then these trees were planted by God," they said.

They wanted to tell us about God. That is why they worked hard over the words, then told us how God made trees.

To hear so many things mixed me up. When I heard about Jesus, I thought Mpawachi and Monchanki had come from God's house. I thought, Probably the thing to do is to follow God. But I was a little bit sad. Wait and think about this first, I thought.

Monchanki and Mpawachi did not know the words very well, but they kept telling us something. I said, "What are they saying that about? Let them talk on! They just bother me with their talk. Who could enjoy listening to that?" I went to my brother, Tsowinki's, house. He lived just one bend downriver on the Pushaga. He had asked me to come and drink. I did not have any sense then. Now when I tell about it, I am ashamed.

Why did I make our sisters suffer? I went off where the drums were going *teen, teen, teen*. I drank with my brother, Tsowinki, then I said, "Come to my house to drink." While we were drinking *masato* the people began to fight at my house. The girls were afraid.

Lorrie says of the incident: "Our fear was that they would kill each other. We begged the Lord to spare their lives until they could hear the Gospel—and He heard our prayer. We just went down into a hollow nearby where any stray bullets flying around would not have reached us. Most of them had spears and machetes. There was a great clashing of metal."

Then Irina said, "Look! The girls have run away. They told you about God, and now they have run away."

I was sad. I said, "Why did they do that?"

My wife scolded me and said, "Stop drinking here! Why do you do this to the poor girls? You have no sense doing this. Go and drink far away if you want to get drunk. We made our poor sisters suffer. Before they really know how to speak Candoshi, we made them suffer."

"That is enough," I said, "no more drinking. No more fighting around here. No more shooting. What if a bullet should hit one of them? We will go get them."

The next day we got the girls and they came back.

Mpawachi said, "Come here, brother." And I thought to myself, What is she saying that for? I wonder what she wants? But she wanted to tell me a little bit of God's Word. She said, "I prayed for you. I talked to God when you got very drunk." When she said that, I was ashamed.

"Why did we do that?" I said. "That is bad, that is ugly. We drank bad." We talked among ourselves and I said to Mpawachi, "If I die, I will just die alone. The buzzards will eat me. Let the buzzards eat me."

Then Mpawachi said, "No, brother, God will help you. You will not die."

So that is what I thought about.

The girls suffered very much. They were both sick and lay there moaning. At first we did not know what was the matter and we said, "Why are they doing like that?" Day after day passed and they did not eat. But God helped them. If God had not helped

them, two *kirinko* would have died among us, Monchanki and
Mpawachi. In our country there is lots of malaria. That is why
when they came to live with us they got it. Now when I think of
that I say, "Why did they suffer like that?"

We worked hard with them and little by little they knew more
words.

Then Mpawachi said, "Now I will tell you about God." I could
hardly wait. She said, "Jesus is the One who died. He cleanses us
with His blood." I stood with my mouth open. As she kept telling
us God's Word, I said, "Really? So that is what God is like!" My
heart was happy when the girls told me about God.

> *After nearly two years of writing the Candoshi language
> phonetically and analyzing the intricate grammatical struc-
> ture, the women made preliminary attempts at Bible transla-
> tion. Tariri was delighted when they arranged the words of
> the first verse of Scripture and tried it out on him. He was
> further pleased when they sang to him a little chorus they had
> been translating. With his help they revised it and wrote more
> verses.*

When I laughed, Monchanki and Mpawachi looked into my
eyes and knew that I understood.

"What are you thinking?" they said.

They were learning to talk and I was happy. I said, "When you
tell me God's Word, my heart is happy."

"Is that the way you feel, brother?" they said, and I said, "Yes."
Mpawachi and Monchanki were happy, too. They said, "Let us
sing!" So we sang a little. We could not sing well, but they could
not teach us well. That is hard work. We sang a little at first, and
they taught us God's Word.

We began to know. I thought a lot in my heart and said, They
must be telling the truth, and I was scared. We had never heard
before, and they told us God's Word. If only I could teach them
all the words! Then we could know well.

Later, more of us gathered together. We sang a little bit. We made a lot of noise together.

They told us about Jesus dying on a tree. So that is what they want to tell us? I thought. They even talk about a dead person. They told us a little bit, and then a little bit more. Monchanki told me Jesus died to pay for the bad things we did. They speared Him and made Him suffer. Blood and water came out of his body. He died. Then they laid Him in a cave. If He did that, why should we not love Him? we said.

After awhile Old Shotka came. I talked with him.

"That is what God's Word says," I explained.

"Really?" he said. "So that is why the girls came. They came to tell you about God."

I told him all I knew.

"It is true, brothers," Old Shotka said. "Let us believe that. I will remember this and love God, too."

He had never heard before, but he listened well to God's Word.

VII

We Love Tiyotari

In 1952 when Doris Cox went to the United States for furlough, Rachel Saint accompanied Lorrie Anderson in the Shapra tribe. Tariri gave her the Indian name Tiyotari. She made good progress in the language and was able to assist in the translation of Bible stories and in teaching the Shapras before she went to the Auca tribe of Ecuador.

The following letters from Rachel picture the significant parting of the language curtain in Chief Tariri's domain:

Yarinacocha Jungle Base
April 11, 1952

Dear Folks:

Just a note to share with you the good news that I have been given a tribal assignment. I will leave the Base about May 15 for the long flight to the Shapra Indians with Lorrie Anderson. This trip will be about five hours in our JAARS plane, and then seven or eight hours upriver by canoe.

Pioneering in the tribe was hard work. The Indians were not ready to accept strangers. Over the months their resistance has been broken down until now Chief Tariri himself refers to the girls as his sisters and himself as their brother. The girls could not think of leaving for furlough together and perhaps come back to find the Indians scattered in the deep jungle.

My personal interest for some time has been in this Can-

doshi group of Indians in the north jungle. I had wanted to go to the Muratos, but found later that they speak a dialect of Shapra. Since there was no available partner to go to a new tribe with me, I gladly offered to fill in with the Shapras during the girls' furloughs.

The situation is monolingual and one learns the language the hard way. Some time before they left the tribe the girls were compelled to try to translate a few verses of Scripture even though they felt inadequate. An Indian woman lay dying, and there was no one else to tell her of Christ. The girls feel that perhaps there was a response and that as a result of the first verses translated, there is a Shapra soul in heaven.

The girls' reports of the tribe make one eager to help out in the work. Lorrie tells of how the people have won their hearts—especially the Chief, a real leader and a man who loves his wife and children.

Lorrie was talking to him one day about the Indians of our country. They used to go on the warpath, she told him, but they do not do it anymore. They used to kill with a tomahawk or bow and arrow, and then they scalped their victims. Tariri thought for awhile and then he said, "We Shapras do not do it that way." He launched into an explanation of the process of head-shrinking, the details of which I will spare you. "That is the way the Shapras do it. That is good. That is good," he said. Lorrie said she wondered what it was good for, so she asked him. He said that it was good to hang the shrunken head in your house and drink and dance about it. "It is very pretty," he added. He would not admit having ever done it, but said that the Huambisas do. Dave Beasley, our translator among the Huambisas, says that they say they do not hunt heads, but the Shapras do!

Is this enough of the picture to show you that we will be needing your prayers as we go?

> *In Him, "Whose we are and Whom we serve,"*
> *Rachel Saint*

Shapra Land
Pushaga River
July 1, 1952

Dear Folks:

We are now settled among the Shapra Indians on the Pushaga River which is not far from the Ecuadorian border. I wish somehow I could introduce you to our Indians. They would look at you squarely in the eye for a long time until they were satisfied, and you would find yourself looking at them too. The men have long wavy black hair with bangs cut to the eyebrows, wrap-around skirts, and red paint carefully applied to be decorative. They would jab their spears in the earth at your door or carefully place a blowgun on your front porch when they come to visit because they know that you are their friend. Their wives come along too, with a baby or two tied on front or back, and they bring their bananas and yuca with them in canoes.

The Shapras are likable Indian folk—handsome too, especially when they get their bright feathers out and comb their hair and primp and paint up. We find in them a character that we respect. We find it hard to believe that our Chief has avenged the killing of two of his brothers; that a pretty little young wife choked her first baby to death after her first husband died. She wanted to marry again but no one would take her while she had the baby to care for.

This jungle is a dream of nature's beauty—but a red sunset or rainbow here means certain death for someone, and the call of a certain bird is an ill omen. At night when the men have to be away, the women come with their children and sleep on the floor beside us. They are afraid of the evil spirits. Although we cannot tell them much yet, they know we are not afraid and they feel safe with us.

Last Sunday we went on a canoe trip to Shimpotka's place, a huge palm-thatch house with quarters for each of two wives.

Along the way we had to get out on a huge fallen tree which blocked the passage of our big canoe. The men got slippery bark and skidded the canoe across the tree. Coming back, the men had to strip to their shorts and finally get in the water and pull the canoe over this same tree. As the evening star shone in the fading sky, we once again reached the big Pushaga stream on which we live. "This is my water," said the Chief, meaning that he ruled it and the Shapra Indians whose huts dot its banks. He loves it. It is his home, and they are his people. But he turned to us and said, "Monchanki, [that's my partner], Tiyotari [that's me], come and let this be our water!" It was a generous invitation, and Tariri himself does not know all that is involved in it. He only knows that our lives are different; we have peace and do not always fight and kill. Once before he had invited the girls to live here—and to die here. For the Lord's sake we want it to be "our" water. But most of all, because the Savior died to redeem these Shapra friends, we want it to be His water.

To tell them so, we need His Word in their language; and to write it, we must live and learn day by day, word by word, phrase by phrase. There is no other way to do it, for there is no intermediary language.

In Him, "Whose we are and Whom we serve,"

Rachel

Shapra Land
Pushaga River
July 19, 1952

Dear Folks:

I am holding in my lap a cute little round-eyed Indian baby about six months old, clothed only in his coppery brown skin and little strands of red and blue beads on his fat little wrists and ankles. Yesterday, I awoke from a siesta to the mournful wail of the Shapras. I had been vaguely aware that a woman had come with her baby and was sitting on our floor with the little one in her lap. Lorrie was there so I went back to sleep only to be startled awake by that heart-rending rhythmic cry accompanied by Shapra words repeated over and over in an agonized voice. I still cannot understand the words, but the intonation I knew accompanied only fear or grief.

I went over to the mother as she wailed. The baby had had four convulsions and was burning up with fever, and there was no response from his eyes. They might have been glass eyes, without even the motion of a doll. I was not sure that there was any life until I felt the pulse. Poor Indian mother! No wonder she wailed, for she too thought the child was dead.

We felt we must work immediately to bring the temperature down (it was 104), but before we could do anything the mother was crying to Tariri, talking of witchdoctoring. She had come for tobacco (over which they chant to the evil spirits) and yet she had come to our house. We were nonplused. What a conflict! Knowing what we had was good, yet she was afraid to break with the evil spirits. And our Chief was agreeing to get the tobacco and chant to the boa for the baby! That was disappointing too. As Lorrie tried to persuade the mother to let her give the baby medicine, I gave the little fellow a sponge bath, not understanding the mother's words that with tobacco one must not give anything else. If they chanted, we could not give medicine, she said—and she chose the way of the tribe. If they gave tobacco we would have no part in it, we told her. They must not give it on our porch. Without immediate help the child would likely die.

It seemed a hopeless situation. We prayed. Call the Base doctor on the radio, seemed to be God's answer. Perhaps the Indians would listen to the doctor's word since he had recently helped them here with the medical clinic.

I put in an emergency call which was answered immediately. How we thanked God for a Christian doctor at the other end! Give the aspirin anyway, he said. The mixture with tobacco juice would do no harm. But the mother would have none of it. If the chanting didn't work, then we could give the medicine. But that would be too late.

Lorrie stood sadly by, the aspirin lying where she had left it. She had seen our Chief go to his platform to chant over the tobacco, imploring the boa to take away its curse, as he whiffed the tobacco up his nose. He had said that in this way his child had been healed. Though he knew our opposition, he had gone, and though he knew we had offered medicine, he had offered to chant! Lorrie was stunned, for it seemed that he was beginning to accept some of our teachings. But he too knew the baby was dying, and in his desperation he had turned back to the only way he had known.

But the mother had carried the babe many hours in burning sun over jungle trails to our door. If witchdoctoring had been her first thought, why had she come to us?

I felt we must not stand idly by. We could hear Tariri's chanting, while the baby's condition grew graver by the minute. I urged Lorrie to go over and talk to the Chief—to remind him that when his wife lay at death's door, he permitted us to nurse her back to health with medicine. He himself had asked God to spare her life, and God had done it, without tobacco, or chanting, or invoking the spirits. She went over and started to talk to his wife, reminding her that aspirin had taken her fever down. Finally the Chief left his chanting to come out from behind the net (where he had hidden in shame to do it) and talked.

I was amazed at the Chief—his eyes were like those of a drugged person. I spoke to him sternly. We had given aspirin to his wife, I reminded him. Why should not the child have it now before it was too late? He agreed finally that we could give the aspirin first. But Lorrie stood her ground—not if they were going to chant, too. I went to crush the aspirin and put it in an eye dropper. When I got back to the house, the mother let me give the aspirin, and the Chief helped to hold the baby's mouth open.

It would be only a step in his healing, we knew that—but God's power was at stake. We would have been just as sure of His ability to heal the child without the medicine, but it had been given in His name.

The mother returned to our house and let Lorrie bathe the baby. Then she wept in relief.

A half hour later the baby was amazingly better, and shortly the Chief, who had not returned to his chanting, came to our door to ask how many hours it would be before the baby's fever would go down. "It is down now," we replied. Just then the child woke up—bright-eyed, playful, well! Healed—not by aspirin, but by God Himself—as a sign to a people who for years have had witchdoctors call on evil spirits to cast out sickness.

At 9:30 we were all in bed, the village in peace, the baby sleeping. How different the story would have been except for the victory of the Lord!

"They say God is greater than the boa," we heard them tell each other.

> *In Him, "Whose we are and Whom we serve,"*
> *Rachel*

From our hut on the Pushaga River
December 14, 1952

Dear Folks:

Yesterday afternoon the Indians heard the plane. They left immediately by canoe to meet it at the mouth of the Morona where the water is deep enough for the Aeronca to land. So here goes for a little news to send out with the plane.

We have been back from the Base about a month. When we returned we found the Chief had taken his sick brother over to the Huambisa witchdoctor. Then shortly after we arrived he himself came down with a severe case of flu or malaria—his bones ached and he couldn't hunt, and he talked of going to the witchdoctor. Then his Huambisa friend, Chief Wanka, arrived with several Indians who are part Huambisa, part Shapra, and all of whom know something of chanting to the spirits. Sick as he was, the Chief went on with the fiesta for which he had been preparing. He began to talk louder, and more vehemently, and then to drink masato. As night fell the flares were lit and the fiesta continued with drumming, and dancing by the men. The women stay in the background with the children ready to flee if the men get violent, or start fighting.

We had ringside seats since Chief Tariri's house is not ten feet from ours, and we watched from the shadows. All night long the Chief's wife served the drink, with her tiny baby tied on her back. In the wee hours they decided that Chief Wanka had a sore leg which should be cured. Our Chief got out his tobacco, and a witchdoctor began whiffing great puffs up his nose and mouth. Then going over to Chief Wanka, he performed. Dropping down on one knee, he slithered his fingers along the sore leg, every motion of his body suggestive of the boa they worship. In the shadow and gloom, it took little imagination to see the snake's head as the witchdoctor wriggled and then quickly sucked with his mouth, blowing out the tobacco smoke as he did so. The dum, dum, dum of the drum added to the effect. Except for the deviltry of the thing, it was a good show.

The all-night ordeal made the Chief much worse, and a day later he was telling us he planned to go off with his friends to the strong witchdoctor of the Huambisas. "God says No to witchdoctors," Lorrie reminded him. "If you go you are throwing away God's Word." But he ached all over and decided that he would go along with his friends just this time. "Perhaps if I could see paper for myself, I would not go," he added. It was a sad sight to see our Chief go off in a canoe

*paddled by two of the young boys, his head covered with a
palm leaf to shelter him from the sun. As he went, we realized
the fault was not entirely his, and that he no doubt will believe when he has God's Word.*

"Just twice the witchdoctor will drink ayahuasca, *and then
Tariri will be all better," Chief Wanka had told us. "When I
come back after five sleeps," Tariri said, "I will go hunting
with my blowgun the next morning."*

In Him, "Whose we are and Whom we serve,"
Rachel

Monchanki and Mpawachi told us a lot about God, then sister
Tiyotari came also.

When Monchanki came with Tiyotari she wrote paper day after
day. She wrote God's Word. After that they showed it to me.
Monchanki lived for paper, and Tiyotari, too. At that time I really
began to know God's Word. They told us how Jesus was born.
Then after that they told us again how Jesus was killed, how He
paid for the bad things we did by dying for us, and how Jesus sent
people out to tell His Word. The girls did not just live here; they
suffered until they could write the stories.

One day I said to Monchanki and Tiyotari, "There are people
far away that I would like to show you." I thought, If it is true
that they want to tell God's Word, and that is why they came,
then they will be willing to go, and we will see if they will tell
God's Word up there. So I took them upriver.

But while we were there, I thought about getting drunk. The
people there gave me *masato.* So after I had drunk and drunk and
drunk and I was almost drunk Monchanki said to me, "Let us go.
Do not get drunk here, brother. Do not drink."

I just listened a little bit, and then my wife looked at me, but I
wanted to stay and drink. Then Irina said, "Come on, let us go." So
I left.

I thought, The girls must be telling the truth about God, because
they do not want to stay here where there is lots of *masato.* I

guess they say, If we sleep here, Tariri will get drunk and then he will talk bad. Because of that I began to know why they came to learn Candoshi.

They taught us about Jesus.

They also told us how Jesus spoke to the wind and it became calm. What kind of a person can speak to the wind, and the waves become still? They wrote and wrote. They also told us how Jesus even made the dead alive. What person can make the dead get up again? They also told us about His healing one whose eyes were closed. What person can heal the eyes of the blind? He also touched ones with twisted bodies, the kind of person that lies there helpless. Jesus made even that kind of person get up.

"In God's house you will live well," the girls said. "If you obey Jesus, then it will be good." They told us, and wrote it all down.

In my heart I thought, You are telling the truth. God is always like that. We cannot know everything about Him.

They also told about Jesus walking on the water. What person can do that? Of course the dragonfly can, but God has made it able to do that.

So in the beginning we heard these things. First Monchanki and Mpawachi, and later Tiyotari came and spent all their time working hard on God's Word.

Rachel reported on March 30, 1953:

This year, for the first time, the Shapra Indians have the story of the resurrection. In the last month, Lorrie has been translating with the Chief the story of the death and resurrection of Christ. I heard him telling Shimpotka the story. I wish you all could have heard him as he sat cross-legged on his platform, with his bare chest and his long black hair, but most of all to see the animation in telling that story so new to him. Shimpotka was feathered up and painted, and listened for the first time, along with two Muratos from another part of the tribe.

Tariri said, "When they wanted to kill Jesus, they did just what we used to do before our sisters came." Shapra custom called for a big pow-wow in one of the huge round-end houses to plan definitely the killing raids. Referring to the spearing of Jesus' side, he said, "You see, Shimpotka, away back in those days they used the same kind of spears we use now!"

I translated with little Tsirimpo, in very simple Shapra, the story of the raising of Lazarus, and a few other stories which is all I could attempt. To my great surprise, I found that the story of Lazarus was simple enough for the women and children to understand and memorize. They tell it now, by the light of the moon, to each other. "Didn't he stink?" they ask. "Lazarus, come! Come out of there!" we hear them repeat to each other.

If there is one believer among the Shapras it is little Tsirimpo. One day as I told him again about heaven, he said, "I want to go there. Let us go!"

I began to love Jesus. Who else was like Him? What person could do the things He did?

We loved Tiyotari very much. She played the drums for us, the kind you squeeze and squeeze [accordion].

Tiyotari taught us many things. I said, "How many *kirinko* are coming here! Now there will be enough of them to teach people, for there are many more of our people."

In the beginning I did not tell the girls that I took heads. The *patrón* told me not to. He said, "If you tell them about killing, the soldiers will come and get you." When I heard that I said, "No, I am not going to tell them now. Maybe someday, after a long time, I will tell them." I hid my hair belt. I hid it and I did not tell them about it.

Then one day I told Tiyotari all about how we used to take heads. I told her how the ancestors took heads. She said, "Brother, tell me all of the ancestors' words. What did they do? You tell me." So that is what I did, and we talked and talked.

I told Tiyotari about the *metori*, the bird that tells us what is going to happen. There were many, many Candoshi then. There were many old men and many young men. The married men would ask the *metori* how their wives were living. A man would say, "While I am off hunting, I wonder if some young man comes and sees my wife. While I am off thinking only about game, maybe that is what they are doing. Tell me, *metori*, is that the truth?" Maybe the little bird would say *cheek-awe* [a negative response], and the man would say, "Oh, it is all right then. There is nothing like that going on." Then he happily goes hunting, and brings the birds or animals back home.

But if the little bird said *cheek-ee-cheek-ee-cheek-cheek* [an affirmative response], the man would know what was happening. "That is what your wife is doing," the *metori* would say. He would be furious and say, "No more of that." He would stop right there, whatever he was doing, and take his blowgun and his spear and go home where his wife was. He would say, "Come on, give me some *masato*. Hurry up, hurry up," and he would drink three gourdsful of *masato* and quickly spear his wife to death. "You are very bad. The bird has told me." After that he would put his spear beside him and sing a song.

That is what I told Tiyotari about spearing the wife who saw another man.

With the young men the older ones also had another way. They would stare into their eyes and talk and sing to find out. The young man might be his brother or a male relative. "How do you live?" the older man would ask the young man. Then he would chant to him. If he decided that the young man had been seeing his wife, he would spear him on the spot. If the young man was guilty and he was strong, he might spear the older man first. If the man could stare back and deny everything, the older man would say, "All right. Everything is all right. We will forget it."

When Tiyotari heard about this, she was scared to death. She could not say a word. She was as quiet as if she were dead. She was no doubt saying to herself, Why does brother Tariri say that? Well, I guess it is because it is true. She was no doubt thinking, He might do that to me. Brother Tariri might kill me like that.

We loved Tiyotari very much and gave her things. We stuffed birds and gave them to her.

Then one day Tiyotari said that she was going. I said to her, "Where are you going?" She said, "I am going to teach other people. The name of the people is Auca. I am going to the Aucas, and there I am going to teach." I said to her, "We want you here." She said, "No, I am going to the Aucas to tell them about God. I would like to stay, but I must go to others. I must go to another country to teach, for they do not know God's Word there. Mpawachi will be back soon."

So by that I knew what Tiyotari was doing. And I knew that the girls were teaching the truth. We loved Tiyotari very much and we were sad when she left. We said, "When will we ever see her again?"

Of course she went because God ordered her to go. She must have thought, God will help me. In the place where I go, God also follows. She is not even afraid to go where there is killing. I said to myself, Tiyotari is greater than the men. She is like a chief. She is like a chief among the *kirinko*, she has a heart like a chief. Being strong, she went.

Rachel described her departure in a letter dated April, 1953:

Dear Folks:

Our one-day trip from the tribe to the Base went this way: Up at 3:30 to do last-minute packing and put the pot on the great log fire. Breakfast, the usual delays, the loving farewells to the Indians, and a 6 A.M. departure by dugout canoe with Chief Tariri and his family. Four hours downstream in a heavy drizzle to meet the waiting plane at the big river. An early afternoon stop at a small jungle town to gas up the plane and then the trip over the stretches of "green carpet," broken only by the river highways. We landed at Yarinacocha five minutes ahead of the 6 P.M. deadline—500 miles of easy travel which without the plane would have taken us several months of strenuous river travel.

In recent weeks Lorrie has completed the first translation of the Christmas story and the healing of the nobleman's son. We asked the Chief to tell it back to us on tape in his own words. He said, however, that he couldn't do it. Lorrie patiently went over it with him again, explaining how the lad was healed by the word of the Lord alone although He was many miles away from the boy. Tariri finally agreed to try only when we assured him we could erase it if it were not well done. The result? A bit of God's Word in Shapra with the additional comment: "When we, in a long time, throw out the witchdoctors, we will tell our children it is because our sisters came and taught us that Jesus is greater."

Pray that soon there will be believers here among the Shapras.

In Him, "Whose we are and Whom we serve,"
Rachel

VIII

Jesus Came into My Heart

My sister Mpawachi talked much with me. As soon as she knew our language she always taught me what God said. "When one lives a bad life, it is never good," she said. "People who steal are bad. It is very bad to steal. It is just as bad to lie.

"Hating is also bad," she said. "God's Word says that hating is not one bit good. He says that loving everyone is good. You should love your brothers and cousins, your uncles, even your neighbors and friends as though they were your brothers. Killing is not like that. Killing is bad because God said, 'Do not kill, whether they are your relatives or your neighbors.' Stop it!" What does one gain by killing? After we think about killing, we hate our neighbors and go out to kill each other. Because of this God will punish us very much.

He will put those who kill into darkness. One's eyes unable to see will always make one lose the way. It is like walking in a fog. You cannot make out anything. It is no use to try to find your way in the darkness because you will always be falling. It is terrible to be lost like that. That is where the people who do not love God will live.

At first Mpawachi asked me to help with some words. She wanted to say them easily and did not want to forget them. "When we have worked out these words together," she said, "then I will tell you longer stories about God. But help me with the words first.

I do not say some of these things too well." And that was right. We laughed about it a lot together.

At first I just taught her a lot, before my heart was changed. After I taught her awhile, she asked me, "What is the word for 'understanding'? What is the word for 'heart'?" Then I gave her the word for "dirt" and "dirty." So she said, "That is in you, in your heart. That is what your heart is like."

Then she asked, "What is it inside your flesh that comes out?" So I said, "Blood." She took a piece of paper and said, "What is this like?" And I said, "It is white, and there is no dirt on it." She asked how to say, "Throw something behind your back." So she threw away a stick and said something about throwing away dirt, throwing away the bad. "Do that," she said. "Throw away the dirt and say 'no' to the devil. Tell him to get behind you." She said, "How do you say, 'Live happily'?" I taught her how to say, "To be kept back by something." She wrote all of it down on paper. I taught her many things, and would say, "That is good" or "Just throw that out, you cannot use it."

They keep telling and telling about God, I thought. When they tell a lot then they say, "God says, 'Receive Jesus.'" I wondered about Jesus. What shall I do? What shall I do? Shall I leave killing? Shall I stop fighting? If I leave fighting, people will not think I am a chief any more.

I thought, What do I want to do with my life? I want to be greater than all people. I will make myself greater than all other chiefs. Then everybody will fear me and I will be happy. I want to live by myself with nobody to bother. I should have killed everyone. Then I could go anywhere without any worries and work as I like. Without anyone around, who would care what one did? Or who would live next to one to be a bother?

That is how I thought, not knowing what to do. Then I thought, What am I saying? After awhile I thought, That is what I will do. I will love God.

I had already decided in my heart about God, but I was not thinking about it as I came home from hunting, running along in my ragged skirt. I was thinking only about food. In my ragged skirt and my dartholder over my shoulder, I came home. Mpawachi called, "Brother, come here. Come quickly." I thought, Why? Why is she saying, "Come here, brother"?

I put my blowgun down and went with my dartholder still over my shoulder. I said, "What, sister? What is this all about?" I will listen first, I thought. Then I will hang up my dartholder. "I have not even had a bath yet," I said.

"That does not matter," she said.

I was ashamed. There was dirt all over me, even on my cheeks. I was dirty from having been so far away, and there was monkey blood on my back where I had carried the spider monkey after shooting him with the blowgun. I looked like a child who had no mother. So I sat down like that, with my dartholder over my shoulder, and Mpawachi began to tell me God's Word.

She said, "Brother, when are you going to receive Jesus? Receive Him right now."

I said, "All right." My heart was so happy when I said, "All right." I received Jesus with my ragged skirt on, without even having had a bath. Then we talked with God.

When I talked with Jesus I said, "You cleanse me with your blood. Put good in my heart. My heart is dirty. Throw all the dirt away. I will follow only you. I want to follow in the same path with you. I do not want to live bad any more. Take out everything that holds me back. Throw it far away. Send it away."

When I said that, Jesus came into my heart.

A letter written by Doris Cox to Cameron Townsend, Director of the Wycliffe Bible Translators, provides backstage illumination for the dramatic turning point in Tariri's life:

September 17, 1953

Dear Uncle Cam:

We have a date marked on our calendar, September 9 —2:45 P.M. "Tariri accepted the Lord." Probably never again in my life will I have an experience like that. Knowing the Shapras and the history of our time here, you know all it means.

During the fiesta three days before Tariri had said, "I am not a drunkard; I am just having a good time. When we accept God's Word, we will leave drinking completely." I wondered what was keeping him from accepting, and decided that translating some Scripture verses with him would help. But he was busy, and I didn't see how I could possibly do the verses I wanted to. I didn't feel like translating, but I went ahead on Hebrews 9:27 and John 1:12. When I see how Scripture in his language opens his eyes, my faith is strengthened and I'm reminded of what he said over a year ago when he listened to the very first verse that had ever been translated into the Candoshi language: "When you talk like that, my heart leaps with understanding."

And so it was that on that hot afternoon when I wasn't equal to the task of bringing a heathen chief to Christ, the "Word of God quick and powerful, sharper than any two-edged sword, piercing even to the dividing asunder of soul and spirit and a discerner of the thoughts and intents of the heart," made his hunter's eyes intent with understanding. I don't know who suggested it first—it hardly needed to be said. Tariri was thinking of accepting Christ, and the question was—on his part—when could he?—on mine, when would he?

Tariri gave me the phrase, "Do you want to receive Jesus into your heart?" I didn't know exactly how to say it, because never before has that question been asked of a Candoshi Indian! He waited till I had written it down, and I read it back to him for approval. It didn't come. He said instead, "I want very much to receive Jesus into my heart, Mpawachi. I will not say, 'no,' at all." So he was born again!

He went home, told his wife and children, and a few minutes later, the oldest boy, Tsirimpo, came over to be saved. I had to do more explaining to him, and the Lord helped me to speak fluently on a subject that had both Lorrie and me tongue-tied before I went home on furlough.

Both give every evidence of the new birth. We hear Tariri praying at night and before meals. He witnesses continually, urges everyone to come around to hear God's Word, asks me to teach him, so he will know a great deal soon. The problem of drinking parties is a big one for him. The Huambisa chief is coming over. Tariri will also be entertaining the Muratos who can't live without their strongly fermented masato; *and he will be visiting in their wild territory.*

Tsirimpo loves to tell that he is God's child; that his name is written in the Book of Life, and that his sins are forgiven. His face lights up, and he says his heart is happy. He has brought a young playmate around to be taught and urges him to accept Jesus. "However," he warns his father, "do not urge too much. He does not understand yet. We had to hear again and again before we accepted."

Irina, the chief's wife, and perhaps half a dozen others have expressed a desire to accept Christ, and the interest is great on the part of most who listen.

Every day Tariri is here I have been working with him translating verses, or explaining them to him. Tonight we translated I Peter 5:7 and Romans 5:8 and we discussed I John 1:9, John 14:2, 3, and I Peter 2:2, 3. Irina was present also, listening with great interest. Tariri asked, "What would happen if I killed a man? Would I still be God's child?" "Yes," I told him, "but God would punish you severely." "And what about the men I killed in the past?" he asked. "That is forgiven. Jesus paid your debt," I said. His moment of doubt passed. "I have no desire to kill," he said. He wants to know many things. He understood tonight that he will grow as a Christian by feeding on the Word. (I Peter 2:2, 3.) I have more respect for the Scripture all the time!

In His Wonderful Name,
Doris

At night lying there I would think in my heart, I have now received Jesus. Having done that, what shall I do? Shall I live right? Shall I leave my bad life? I will.

Now that I know God I say, Why should one be against God? I cannot any more. Before, I did not worry about being bad. My heart was dirty. Like a wild boar that rolls in the dirt and gets dirty all over, that is what I was like. I rest my heart in God now. Why should we not love Him?

When Jesus comes back, what will I do? What will I say? I am not good enough to talk to Him. I am a chief, but my feet are on the ground. If God should make the earth turn to water and throw down fire upon us, even a chief could not send it back. How could you send it back if God sent down His anger upon the earth? That is why I think much in my heart now. That is why I say, I will love God very much.

The Peruvian general in Iquitos sent Tariri a letter, asking for information about the work of the American women.

At Iquitos, the largest city of the jungle, is the major government outpost in Amazonian Peru. Tariri could not write. He dictated the following letter in Candoshi and it was translated into Spanish:

I send God's Word. I write about God and send it. Even though I am a chief, I live well now.

The *kirinko* do not just live here. They teach us God's Word. The very things they taught us stayed with us, and then we knew.

At first they could not speak well, but they kept telling us and we came to love Jesus. I had just begun to know God's Word, but I received Jesus. I thought, I want to be greater than everyone. But then Jesus came into my heart.

Though I love Him, I am still a chief. God makes one a great chief.

My name is Tariri. Even though I am a great chief, I love Jesus. I do not want anyone to doubt it.

IX

God Keeps Me from Revenging

"We will even shoot the señoritas." That is what Old Shotka had said. We were talking about that and I said, "But they tell us about God. Why would you want to kill anybody like that?" I already loved God when I said that.

Then the upriver people deceived me. Old Shotka, their chief, Pirocha, Pincho, and Young Chiriapa deceived me. Old Shotka's nephew Shimpotka ordered them, they say.

"Let us trade boar and jaguar skins," they said at first. Having cured the skins, they all came to trade with me. I gave them cloth. I thought they really wanted to trade, so I told them to get more skins. Old Shotka said to me, "We will come again."

When Old Shotka did not come when we expected him, Shimpotka came to see me. "Where is Uncle Shotka?" he said. "They should have come a long time ago." I thought, Why does he say that?

But Shimpotka deceived me. They had gone first to visit Shimpotka in order to deceive me.

After that while we were gathered together in peace, they came.

The sun had come out bad that day. It was dark, and the sun was dim and it was cold. I thought of my *chacra*. Now when I have finished clearing, I thought, I will plant peanuts and other things.

I had asked my brother-in-law Old Chiriapa to come over. He came real early to my house. Then Shotka and his crowd came to Old Chiriapa's house, but when they looked they found it was empty. He had left. So they said, "Where is he? He is probably at his brother-in-law Tariri's house. Well, there is nothing to do about it. Let us go to Tariri's."

Pirocha said to Old Shotka, "I will shoot Tariri, Father, since you love him and would not want to."

"No," said Old Shotka, "we older ones will shoot him together."

Then Pincho said, "I will kill Old Chiriapa."

Suddenly we heard the sound of a cow's horn being blown. *Po-o-o-o, po-o-o, po-o*, it said. "Who is that?" I said. "It must be Old Shotka. It must be the one who said he was coming."

Along they came, floating down the river. They were not paddling. They did not seem to be in a hurry. There was one skin lying in the canoe. After this I will know that that is the way people do to deceive. Then, I did not know. Irina came running and said, "Are they not deceiving you? Maybe they are coming to kill." That is what my wife said. She made me see what they might do. I said, "Maybe they are coming to kill, but would my own father's relative kill me? But God will help me." I put shells in my gun in case they were coming to kill. Then I said, "Why would they want to kill me?" My brother-in-law Chiriapa was standing behind me. I thought about myself, Afraid of his own relative, he puts shells in his gun. So I took the shells out and put them in my pocket. Then I sat down.

Arosa [Old Shotka's daughter, married to Old Chiriapa] said, "I am going to get water at the river and see my brothers."

Then they came running up the hill, and Arosa followed behind her father. The next time someone does that I will know someone is deceiving me.

Pirocha and Pincho came up and said, "How are you, brother? How are you?" "I am here, I am here," I said. "Sit down." Then I said to Old Shotka, "Come in," and he said, "How are you, brother?" "Sit down," I said. But they did not sit down. I looked in their eyes and could see that they were very excited. I said to my little boy, "Look out! Go away!"

When I said that, they pointed their guns at me. Two of them stood facing me, and two faced my brother-in-law Chiriapa. Just then the guns clicked at me. They were pointing their guns right at me to shoot me, but the guns just clicked. They did not explode. God spared me. Because of God's protection the guns did not explode.

They grabbed their guns and pointed them at me again, saying, "*Ch-ch-cha!*" Then I came to my senses, but as I reached in my pocket for my shells there was the sound of *ste-ee! bang*! They had grabbed my brother-in-law Chiriapa, and all of them were wrestling with him. My attention was fixed on him and not on myself when all of a sudden *ste-ee!* again. My heart tingled as the bullet struck. But God threw it off to one side. If God had not wanted to spare me, they would have killed me.

I thought, God let it all happen to me to punish me for the ones I had killed. God said, You try it and see how it feels. What do you think of the pain?

I felt a pain and groaned. My heart went thud. And at my back I heard the gun, *ste-ee!* That is the way it went. So I ran away as fast as I could.

Pirocha was following me. I could hear his footsteps behind me. I kept running and at the edge of the clearing I fell. My heart went *toom!* What is the matter with me? Then I got a burst of energy. God probably lifted me up as I was being followed. When God made me stand up again, I made another dash. The blood was pouring out of my nose and I kept throwing up blood. At that point God caused Pirocha to turn back. He sent Pirocha back the way he came. He had gotten frightened. He must have thought, Tariri might be hiding, ready to shoot me as I come along.

I ran again and then came to Tanchima's *chacra*. I said there, "Shotka shot me. Why should my own relative shoot me? I am going to the *patrón's*. If I die, I die. God is looking after me." So I prayed, "Father, help me." Even away off there I remembered to pray.

I was not able to breathe. I just gasped and groaned and made strange noises.

I ran again and came to brother Tsowinki's house. I told him that I wanted to go and get medicine at the *patrón's*, so he took me downstream in the canoe. When we got there, the newly picked cotton was piled up in his house. I was crying and moaning with pain. He gave me some camphor to drink, and I felt better. They rubbed some medicine on me.

I sent for Wanka, chief of the Huambisas, to come. So my friend Wanka and his men came to where I was. But he said, "Friend, you will die. How could you get better?" When he said that, my heart was very sad. "If God helps me, I will get better," I said.

When Tariri's Huambisa friends heard of his plight, they reported to David Beasley. He sent a radio message to Yarinacocha where Doris and Lorrie were working intensively on Candoshi language problems. They immediately arranged a JAARS mercy flight to help Tariri.

I cried very much. I prayed a lot.

So God helped me, and our own sisters came and took me to Yarinacocha. There they made me better. That is why I say that God is great. If God had not helped me, I would have died.

I had been angry and thought, I want to kill all the upriver people. But God said, No. So because I was kept from doing it, they still live. God won.

I was never like this in the old days. I was powerful, and I was always angry. Being angry, I thought a lot about killing. Because I used to kill that kind of people, news gets around about me now. "It is because Tariri loves God that he does not come to kill us," they say. "It is as if there were no Tariri. Even though Tariri was a killer, God changed him."

After attacking Tariri's group, the upriver people fled to the Siquanga River area. Later, the elder Tsowinki who had relatives in Tariri's group came downriver with a trader. He passed Tariri's settlement and was seen by some of the downriver Shapras who wanted to retaliate.

"Old Tsowinki is coming!" they cried.

"Let us kill him," said brother-in-law Shiniki and Tanchima. But they were afraid. They said, "Let us wait until brother-in-law Tariri comes."

I had gone out to get palm heart. God probably sent me. Having already received Jesus, I went to get palm heart with Irina. When we came back they said, "Now is our chance. Let us kill him." The young men also said, "Let us shoot him!" Tsirimpo and young Shiniki grabbed their guns and said, "Father, we want to shoot him, but we are afraid."

Loving God, I still followed Old Tsowinki of the upriver group. We said, "We will kill him." But I thought about God. In my heart I said, No, then, Maybe. Having said I would leave killing, should I lie? I am going to love God. After I had said I will love God very much, I left killing. Having done that, should I say, I will become more of a chief by killing again?

We were following Old Tsowinki on our side of the Morona River. He had by then run away downriver on the Morona. His wife had been paddling downriver, and she picked him up in the canoe and took him across to the other side, where he disappeared into the woods. We thought in our hearts, If only he were on this side of the river, the young boys could shoot him. I scolded my brother-in-law Shiniki and said, "You are probably afraid. Why did you not shoot him when you had the chance?" I hesitated in my heart. What shall we do? Is this the thing to do? Should we kill him? What about my having received Jesus? Having done that, should I kill?

I was sad. "Anyway, let us follow them," I said. "The soldiers will get them. Let us have the soldiers take them. Only two of us who are not afraid will follow them."

The next day while it was still dark, when the moon was going down, we got into the canoe and hurried away. Just above Pucucura stream we caught up to them. Old Tsowinki patted his head [a Shapra gesture of despair] and cried, *"Ee-ee-ee!"* The children cried, "They have come to kill us!"

"Wait," we said. "Let us go talk to the soldiers downriver [at the government outpost].

The patrón *Arturo joined Tariri downriver and went with him to the outpost to accuse Old Tsowinki and the others who were of the group that had killed Tariri's brother-in-law, and had attempted to kill Tariri.*

So I said to Arturo, "Let us go!"

"All right," he said, shaking and full of fear. He was very much afraid of me.

When we arrived the lieutenant said, "Let us take them, for the downriver Shapras say, 'These are the ones who killed our people.' " As we talked on the beach the soldiers said, "Bring up Arturo. He is probably the one who ordered the killing. You are the one who sold them the bullets. Why did you sell them bullets?"

We caused Old Tsowinki and Kamposoro to be taken into custody, and the soldiers took them away. As we brought them up on the beach they cried, "*Ee-ee-ee!*" Old Tsowinki and Kamposoro cried. Mikaya, Old Tsowinki's wife, and the children cried to see them go. They made a loud noise. They were trembling.

We said to the soldiers, "Guard them here. Do not let them run away." So they guarded them. The soldiers did not sleep all night, guarding them.

Old Tsowinki and Kamposoro kept crying and saying, "Do not kill us."

"Why should we kill you?" I said. "We are not killing you. We are just punishing you. Now then, live well. Do not be afraid. Because of God we cause you to be taken, and no more. I have decided not to kill you. All of you did the killing. That is bad. Why did you come to the house?"

Old Tsowinki then trembled all over and said, "I did not mean to kill. I only followed along after the others to make sure your children did not get killed."

I said, "After this, stay at home where you belong. Why should you come thinking of killing?" Saying that, I left him alone.

We talked again with the lieutenant. He said, "If they were the real killers, we would send them to our chief downriver. But since they are not, they can stay here. We will just punish them here."

So I said to the soldiers, "I will take them to my place."

I took care of Old Tsowinki and Kamposoro at my place. Old Tsowinki went hungry for a long time. I thought, Let him go hungry. Let him suffer for punishment. We did not kill him. We did not think of killing.

At first I scolded Old Tsowinki to punish him. He was afraid of us. "Tariri is a great chief now," he said of me.

We kept giving them food. I myself did that. Doing that, we loved them. What am I doing? I thought. But this is what God says to do. Giving them food, I would say, "Do not be afraid, you will return home again."

Kamposoro would cry. He cried a lot. "I will never see my mother again," he said. "I will die here for sure."

"No," I said. "You killed our people, but you will not die here, for you yourself did not do the killing."

So we talked and talked to them for about two months and told them about God's Word. We said, "We are doing this because we love God." After we said that, Old Tsowinki's heart was a little bit happy. He began to eat. He had gone a long time without eating, and now we felt sorry. He had learned his lesson.

After about two months, when the moon was at mid-sky, Old Tsowinki said with tears, "Let me go home. Tariri, let me go."

"All right," I said. "Maybe you have learned your lesson. Tell everybody upriver the things that I have been telling you."

Having said that, I took him again to the soldiers. I said, "Tsowinki wants to go home."

"All right," the lieutenant said, "but come back in so many days."

Old Tsowinki said, "All right, I will be back soon." But he did not mean it. He just said that.

So we sent him home to Siquanga, and that was that. They happily paddled away. Kamposoro said, "Thank you, Tariri."

We loved Old Tsowinki because of God. In my heart I said, Since I received Jesus, why should I kill? Let him live happily. Let him return home and live. Who would feed his children? "I have lots of children," he had said. "If I die, who would feed my children?" I thought in my heart, That is true. So scolding him, I sent him away. That is what you do when you know God. You love. That is the way it was.

X

God Tests Me

When my little boy Totarika was just a baby, I thought I would test God. So I killed a tapir. When I shot it my wife said, "My child will be harmed. What shall I do?" But I wanted to try and see what would happen. "What will God do?" I said. "I have received Jesus. Do we not love God?" The ancestors had said that it would harm the child. But Irina gave him vitamin drops every day, and that helped him to stay healthy. And so even though I had killed a tapir, my child grew up.

But God tested me when our baby boy became sick. He was just old enough to crawl. I had been so happy to have another boy, and I suffered much when he became sick. What will we treat him with? I thought. I wanted medicine for him.

When Tariri's infant son had become ill, he broke into the steel drum in which the translators had stored their radio. He assembled the radio and sent a message to Yarinacocha. The translators were dumfounded when they heard his voice coming from the jungle four hundred miles away!

"Send sister Monchanki!" Tariri said. "If the baby dies, we will cry together."

Lorrie said, "Our Base doctor prescribed medicine and told us how to administer it. We passed the word to Tariri and told him how to break into the medicine cabinet. But the next morning Tariri called to say that the baby was worse. We went to do what we could."

The girls came to see our baby. But he died.

The other people said, "If I were the one taking care of them, I would smash all the things they have here."

Irina cried very much. "Even though I received Jesus, God took my child away," she said.

At first I was angry with the girls. I thought, They keep going and going and leaving us, and my baby dies. Then God spoke to me, saying, Do not talk like that. Then thinking in my heart, I said, What am I saying? What am I saying about my child and about the girls? God is just testing me. Why is He?

After that Totarika, who was older, became ill. I had sent him to see the doctor at Yarinacocha. "Go, get taken care of, son," I said. "Your little brother died and we do not want the same thing to happen to you. You, the older one, are not well either. Go, see what can be done about it." I loved my son very much.

Totarika went to Yarinacocha, and we missed him. His mother said, "Let us send for him. I want his company." I said, "All right," and we brought him back. He got sick again here at home. He was grinding rock salt and suddenly gasped with pain. "My vein snapped, Father," he said. It hurt him to breathe. He had sharp pains. He asked his mother to rub him. That was the start of his illness. He just kept having fevers and kept throwing up blood day after day. Finally he died.

Shortly after the death of young Totarika, the seven-year-old son of David and Nancy Beasley in the neighboring Huambisa tribe died suddenly. Tariri and Irina, sympathizing with the Beasleys, were relieved of their own sorrow. Tariri prayed: "Father, I know now that this is one of the things you let happen to people you love."

Then people said to me, "That is what you get for loving God. Look at us. Even though we get drunk, our children do not die. You love God, but your children die. You will not have any sons growing up. It is not worth it to follow God."

If I love God, I thought, He will help me. What will God do? He is probably just testing me. He probably said, What will Tariri do? If I take his children, maybe he will leave me. That is probably why my children died, just to test me.

I thought in my heart about Job. Even though his children died, he did not leave God. He did not throw God's Word away. Why should I?

One day I went to the *chacra* all by myself. There alone in the *chacra* I cried. I cried very much. I prayed to God and I said, What shall I do? If you give me another son, I will be happy. You have given me many girl children. I am tired of looking at girls. I cannot care for that many of them. Why did you give me so many girls? They just cannot live well on their own. They go dashing off here and there, and running off here and there, and get lost.

So I said to God, If you give me another child now, a boy, it will be all right. Why should I leave you?

I had wanted to leave God, and I talked with Monchanki. I thought it was the witchdoctor who had killed my child, and I wanted to kill him. But my sister said, "Wait, brother, let us pray. Let us talk to God about it first."

And then the witchdoctor died suddenly. His heart got real hot and he just ran here and ran there, and he ran and dived into the water to cool off. Then he died.

I prayed to God and I said, You cleanse my heart, Father. I thought about the witchdoctor, and wanted to kill him. I wanted to leave you. Irina also wanted to leave you, God. Now with your help, I will not do that any more.

Then I said to Irina, "God will give us another child. Do not cry so much. Stop crying. My child is in heaven. He is happy there, he is happy with God, and I will see him again someday. You will see him again someday, so do not leave God." So even though I cried very much for my child, I prayed.

Now God has given me another child. Before the baby was born, when I was talking with Irina she said, "My child is a girl."

I answered her, "No, Irina. It is a boy. Did I not pray to God many times about it? I prayed and asked God for two boys. And God said to me, If that is what you want, that is what I will do. God said to me, I will help you. Did God not say that? Then why do you not trust Him? It is a boy."

That night Irina hurt very much. She cried all night. About half an hour before it began to get light, Irina gave birth.

"What is it?" I said.

"It is a boy!" she said.

"Again, another boy!" I said. Oh, I was happy! It is enough, Father, I prayed.

There were some little pills that Monchanki had left and she said, "After Irina gives birth, you give her these pills." I woke Tsirimpo up and said, "Look at the paper and see what it says. How many shall I give her?" [Tsirimpo had learned to read in the Shapra language.] He looked at the paper and it said that she was to have one in the morning and one in the afternoon, so that is what I gave her.

Now our hearts are happy, and that is why I say that God has helped us very much. That is why I say that God is good.

In how many ways has God tried me! One time a cedar log almost crushed me. The log was very big [about two meters in diameter] and it had pinned me down. It was rolling toward my head and I prayed, Father, make the log light. God picked up my head and moved it a little to one side in a small hollow in the ground, and when the log rolled over me it only crushed me lightly. It did not kill me. God is great! He saved me. If my head had been flat on the ground when the log rolled over me, it would have crushed me.

Another time the wind blew so loud I heard it and I started to run. A large rotten tree fell over. It crashed right where I was. But God threw it to one side. We were on the trail, walking one behind the other. It was a very narrow trail, and we were all close together. When I heard the tree begin to fall, I looked to see where I could run. But I could not move. There was someone on the trail in front of me, and the dog was behind. The tree brushed against me as it fell, and killed the dog.

God spared me. Even though the devil wanted to kill me, God said, No, and threw the tree to one side.

Another time I collapsed with malaria, and almost died. How many days did I lie there? But God keeps on sparing me. My book is in heaven. God writes a book for each of us. When you love God He writes a book for you and keeps it. So when He looked at mine, my time was not up yet.

When I was sick with malaria, I also got measles. Again, I almost died. The measles hit me hard. I was burning up with fever. I was already skinny, my eyes were sunken in, and my arms were the size of a fluffy monkey's. I thought, I will not live. But I prayed. I said, Father, that is enough. The measles are killing me. My heart is on fire. It is being cooked. Help me. Chase the measles away. Make me better.

The same day, at noon, I slept. The same day all my fever went down and I became cool. If I loved the devil, he probably would have taken me to be with him long ago.

God does things like that to test us. Who can compare with Him? We human beings are not like that. How could a person save another? He cannot push a tree to one side. He cannot throw something out of the way or send it away, as if it were a dart. Like making a dart fly through the air, God's breath is like that. Like kapok he makes it light and it flies through the air. When something is falling straight and about to crash, can one push it to one side? He even makes heavy bullets fly off in another direction. He blows them with His breath.

For God says, "Wherever you might be, I will follow you there. Every place you go, I follow you. Come on, let us go. I will go with you." God is there. He looks after us.

Another time God spared me from death. I had followed the witchdoctor a little bit. It was probably because of that that God was punishing me. I was thinking about that, the day the witchdoctor had blown on my head, as I walked along. God probably said, Why does he treat me like that again? Why does he not learn?

So I cut my foot that day with an ax. The whole top was chopped off and the blood poured all over. I went to the sister [Beth Hinson, a Wycliffe nurse who made occasional trips to the tribe], and I was ashamed in front of her. I thought she must be saying, Why does he cut himself like that? After I had said a few words, I almost died. I trembled, and everything went black before me. I could not see, I could not hear. I almost died. [Beth asked for a plane to be standing by for an emergency flight to Yarinacocha.] Our sister took care of me and I got better. God punished me only a little bit for having gone to the witchdoctor. He did not want to kill me. I felt better after awhile. At first the cold entered [chill from loss of blood], then my heart felt better.

Why should even a chief say, I am a chief? How can a person be greater than God? God made the earth and put it here for us to live on. He planted food for us, like the *cocona* fruit, and other sweet things. That is why we live strong.

He put the sun in the sky for us to see by. He did many things like that.

We cannot live without Him. We would be like fish drunk with *barbasco* root, not knowing where we are going.

God puts large hearts in us so that we might think. If God had not done that, we would be without sense. Look at the chickens and the armadillos. They have no sense. They wander around, lost. But since God put large hearts in us, why should a person not put the bad out of his heart?

If one knows God, he lives well. I received Jesus. Why should I leave Him?

XI

What I Teach My Children

I do not teach my children about killing. Even though I used to kill, now I say, No, I do not do it any more. I left it and I say no to it, and I do not teach my children about it. If I taught that, it would make us leave God's Word and we would follow the devil. My father had said, "Do it," and all the ancestors taught us those things. We learned to kill so that others would not kill us.

But since the girls came, we have not followed those teachings. Now I say to the people, "Why did I used to be like that? If we are going to kill, we will be killed ourselves. That is bad. We cannot become many that way."

But the Huambisas say, "What is wrong with Tariri? Why does he not go killing any more? At one time he did not sit still." But now, because I love God, I say No. God says not to kill. God has helped me in every way. He has given me another heart. I love Jesus. Why should I think of killing?

Now I teach my children to love God and to go with Him. "If you do not think about God, a snake might bite you," I say.

I teach them about food, too. I teach them how to get palm heart and palm-heart worms, how to split open the tree in order to get them. I teach them to fish with poison, and to hunt. I teach women how to work, and I teach about planting.

I teach the children to pray. I tell them to pray when they go out to hunt. I tell them to say, "God, put out birds and animals for me." I say, "Ask God to help you when you work. Do not just go out, just step out and not even think about God. Ask before you go. Speak to God and say, 'I am going to go out and do such and such.' If you do that, God will help you, and snakes will not bite you. I think God keeps them away when we pray." That is what I tell my children.

"Do not be lazy. Carry water," I tell them. I tell them to cut the weeds in the *chacra*, too. I say, "My sons, what are you going to do when you have a wife? Who is going to feed your wife if you do not know how to work well? When your wife asks for something from the woods, like palm-heart worms, will you just sit around in the house and not do anything? When a woman wants something very much and you do not give it to her, she will be sad. God does not tell us to hate the women. He tells us we should feed them."

Now I do not talk and talk and talk about nothing, as the ancestors did. When my children want to know what the ancestors used to believe and they say, "Who is going to tell me?" then I tell them. I tell them how the ancestors learned to shoot with a blowgun, and how the sun was once a person.

It used to be that when we had a bad dream we would say, "I am going to die." We do not do that now. If we have a bad dream, we tell God. And we say, "Oh, it is nothing. I just dreamed, that is all. God is very great." But our ancestors used to say, "I had a bad dream and somebody will kill me soon." And Old Maama would say, "Then build a house by yourself. If somebody comes to kill you, be strong. You will get the best of everybody else. Run far away. Go off in the woods and live there by yourself, and all of your children will grow up there."

We used to think that when we died, or someone killed us, we would live on the outer edge of the woods and just above the highest trees. We thought we would become birds, the *canishi* bird. It is a little gray bird with a red beak. It comes just before dawn and calls out, *She-she, she-she*, Let us go, let us go. This bird is a spirit bird, and it wants human beings to go with it. So I thought I would become a *canishi* bird and live just above the trees. That is what the ancestors told us. They said we become spirits when we die. The *canishi* bird eats a little wild fruit which is bitter. So I thought to myself, Well, I will have to live on bitterness all the time. That is what the *canishi* bird eats, and if I eat bitterness I will very much became a *canishi* bird.

The ancestors told us that when you die you just forget. When you are still alive you talk and begin to say good-by to people, and you say to your loved ones and relatives, "You stay well. Look after my children. Look after my wife for me. If people try to kill you, kill them back. You punish them." When you have said that, you die, your heart just forgets.

We were very much afraid to die. We talked about it with fear. If we saw a spirit, we were very afraid. We were afraid of the devil, too. We said, "When you die, you leave and do not return ever again. Look! My father and all of his people died and never returned. One after another left, and your heart cannot see them again. They are gone."

Who is there that is not afraid to die? A chief is not supposed to be afraid to die. Chiefs talk and sing about how many they kill and say they are not afraid to die. But when it comes right down to it, chiefs are afraid to die. Even the old ones are afraid.

Now, if you die, you go to be with God. That is what we believe. Your heart will go up, but your body you will leave down here. One is not afraid to die now. But you think of your children. You say, "When I go, who will look after my children?"

My father told me that if anybody was about to die, that person would go and talk to the witchdoctor.

"There are certain diseases for which you should chant," the witchdoctor said. "Then you drink tobacco and when you have chanted, you sleep three nights. After three nights you may drink *masato* and eat everything.

"If your wife has given birth and bleeds a lot, there is another chant."

My uncle told me, "If you want to make your child fat, you chant. You chant about the big frog, the baby golden sloth, and the night monkey. You take the baby early in the morning, before dawn, and chant and chant, then you bathe it in cold water. Then it gets real quiet and sleeps well."

Lorrie comments: "We saw the Shapras bathe a newborn baby with icy water in the early hours of the morning. A mother brought the baby and Tariri chanted for it. She had already lost five or six, and this one died shortly thereafter. We told her, 'No wonder all your babies die.' "

I cannot chant any more. Now we think of medicine, and we talk to God. When my baby gets sick I tell God about it. I say to my baby, "We will use some medicine to make you better." So I give medicine and we say to God, Father, you help the medicine.

I use tobacco to rub on the skin over the liver. I still use tobacco for that, but just for the outside. I do not drink it any more. I also use tobacco for killing worms in the skin [larvae of the botfly which has a tenacious hook]. I think the tobacco makes the worm dizzy, and then you can pull it out.

Our little children do not think about witchdoctors any more. When they used to get sick, they would say, "Father, take me to the witchdoctor. Let us go to him so he can suck and make me better."

Now when the children are sick, they just lie there quietly. Look at my little girl. She got sick at school and Shiniki the teacher brought her home. Her neck was swollen and she went to bed and lay there. God helped her to get better. Now I pray to God and He helps the children get better, and I send them back to school again. I remind them that God is great, and that He Himself wants to make them well. "Do not mix up God and the witchdoctors," I say. "If you do that, God cannot do what you ask Him."

Those who go to school enjoy looking at paper. Now that they are learning paper, they are coming to know God's Word. Some of the older ones cannot learn to look at paper. They make mistakes, but they want paper. Some say, "We are going to try it out first. We will go to school one year and if we cannot do too well, we will still go the next year. Then if we do not do well the second year, we will give it up. It is just because we are old that we cannot do it." But the children's eyes see, they learn the words.

> *Older men are attending school five hours a day with Shiniki, a great sacrifice of time in view of* chacra- *and canoe-making, hunting, fishing, and palm-heart hunting. In the Pushaga location all except one of the older men are now in school. "There really is a big push for learning," says Lorrie, "and we are thrilled with this interest."*

Knowing paper is good for another thing. The outsiders make us suffer. They are always stealing from us, always cheating us. If we know paper, they cannot cheat us any more.

Nearly everybody here goes to school. I said to them, "Do not let the outsiders cheat us. Go to school." Now they think with another mind. Those who look at paper say, "This is what the words say. This is what God's Word says." Then it is possible for them to remember and not forget it. We all love God's Word.

I still do not know how to look at paper very well. When I have learned, it will be easy to tell God's Word. I will be able to say, "This is what God's Word says."

I am very sad about those who live bad. A lot of people lied about me. They kept lying and lying about me. So I kept praying and asking God to help me. Then people stopped believing the lie. I told them how God helped me, and I told them we cannot forget God's Word. I said we should love God very much. God helps me very much. He does not just look on.

As I heard God's Word, I thought, Why did they not come long ago? Why did they wait until now, if they knew God's Word? There were many of the old ones, the ancestors, who wanted to hear.

I asked Mpawachi, "Why did you people not come long ago? If you had told us long ago, the old ones would have known it, too. Why did God give His Book to you, and not to us?"

The ancestors told us many things, about the boa, the toucan, the jaguar, the possum, the ocelot, and the earthquake. These gave *arotama*. I do not tell my children those things. I tell them to talk to God, to talk in Jesus' name.

"God gives you the kind of life by which you will never die," I say. "He gives you *arotama* so that you will be unable to die." In the past, we did not talk to God for life.

When people get old and tired and die, it is just the body that does that. People are not like rocks that just lie there. People are different. When God takes you, you go up to heaven where He is, and you live happily there. You live well there. He gives you a different body. So it is all right to leave behind the old body.

Before, we used to think about boas, and the boas used to call us. Not long ago I was with Irina and as I came along I was listening. A boa was going *doomp, doomp, doomp,* and I said, "I am going to find out for myself." There was the boa, with a little rodent nearby. The boa would lift its head, and then let it fall, and the rodent would lift up its hind end. The little rodent was tame, and the boa was making it more tame. That is the way the boa calls. "I am going to catch that boa," I said. "Maybe he is going to tell me something." I dragged the boa to the canoe. Irina kept saying "No! No! He wants to bite me!" But I said, "No, you hold the vine [tied around the boa] and I will pole the canoe with this stick." The canoe did not want to move. It was against a big thick tree. I poled very hard, but the canoe just kept floating around in the same place. The water just rushed past. Boas grab the water. That is what the ancestors told us. They hold the water back. Then I was angry and I said, "Who is going to bother with this? It is not worth it. The old ones were just deceiving us." So I threw the boa right out of the canoe.

When we would see a red cloud at sunset, we sent the young boys out into the woods. We said, "Look out! The red cloud has been out. That means that *arotama* is in the woods. You go out to sleep in the woods. If you get this power, then when you become very old you will not die."

I used to tell my sons, "When you get married, you will dream about a jaguar. If you get the power of *arotama*, if you dream, then people will not be able to refuse you a wife, but if you do not have that power, they will refuse you. So be sure to dream for a wife, and for children."

We do not go into the woods to sleep for that purpose any more. We do go to the woods to sleep when we want to hunt.

The thing to teach is God's Word, the straight words. The thing to tell is about the life that God gives us, the life by which He takes care of us. When your heart is not right before God, you are living bad. Talk to God. He straightens people out, even the very bad kind.

It is possible for one's bad heart to be cleansed by the blood of Jesus. I teach my children to talk to God. "Cleanse my heart, Father," I tell them to say. All of my children know that. God's Word tells us what to do. God's Word also tells us what not to do.

Three years after the arrival of the translators, Tariri is converted. He renounces his former life of headhunting and superstition for one filled with the love of God and of Jesus Christ.

XII

I Meet the Chiefs of Our Nation

When Tariri first ventured outside his own tribal area in 1955 to take his son Totarika to Yarinacocha for the treatment of repeated fevers, he was invited to go to the capital city of Lima to participate in the official Tenth Anniversary Celebration of the Summer Institute of Linguistics in Peru.

With Lorrie interpreting, Tariri visited the high officials of the nation, including President Odría. He always gave a straightforward account in his own language of his transformation through God's Word. His comments and responses to reporters were unpredictable and refreshing. Upon meeting the president's representative in Lima, Tariri said to him:

It was not long ago that we were living alone and did not know God. But now since the señoritas came to my people, they have told us of Him.

Mpawachi had been living among us for three years with Monchanki. One day when I returned from hunting, she asked me when I was going to become a child of God. Then I received Jesus into my heart.

If the señoritas had not come to tell me the things of God, I would have continued not knowing Him and would still be chanting to the boa. And now I have come to Lima to know you and talk with you. I am happy to talk with the great chiefs of our nation.

I had to come without my wife, but when they asked me, I came. I was happy to come because God wanted to bring me to talk with you.

Surrounded by government officials, and by reporters eager to photograph the jungle chief so exotically arrayed in a combination of tribal garb and warm western clothing to ward off the Lima cold, Tariri met every situation with poise and dignity. In one historic moment, while separated from his interpreters, he felt a strong urge to deliver a message. He did so for fifteen minutes, holding the crowd spellbound by an eloquent speech which no one present could understand! One account reported that "his pronunciation was energetic, accompanied by rare gesticulation and mimicry."

Time *International for July 25, 1955, reported Tariri's meeting with the Peruvian president:*

"His pigtail attractively braided with yellow and orange toucan feathers, a stocky Indian chief and a tall, pale girl from New Jersey dropped in on President Manuel Odría. 'Tamarimta taritamtish no taritamina?' asked Tariri, who is chief of the fierce Shapra tribe in the green-hell upper Amazon basin. The girl, Lorrie Anderson, translated the words into Spanish ('How are you?'). Odría gave the chief a hug. 'Just fine,' he answered. 'And you?'

" 'It is a pity,' Odría went on, 'that we cannot converse in Spanish.' Tariri's answer was as cool as the drizzly weather outside. 'That is your fault. You should have sent us teachers long ago. We never had anyone to teach us until my sister'— he nodded toward Miss Anderson—'came along.' Then Tariri departed for a look around Lima, the first big city he had ever seen. Women's cosmetics impressed him most. 'With us,' he mused, 'it is the men who paint.' "

Following the published interview, Cameron Townsend diplomatically thanked the president for the government's concern with Indian literacy. He expressed appreciation for the bilingual school system in the jungle where members of the Summer Institute of Linguistics were training Indian teachers to educate their fellow tribespeople.

In conversing with educators, Tariri reported with justifiable pride that his young son Tsirimpo and his own younger brother Shiniki were learning to read with a view to becoming teachers in their own tribe.

Tariri gave vivid verbal illustrations of the change which had come to his tribe through Bible Christianity. "Now I do not drink tobacco as we used to do when we chanted. I have ordered my people not to drink it either. I have also told them to stop fighting and to live in peace. This is what God asks."

When it was reported that Tariri could imitate to perfection the songs of more than fifty jungle birds, some of his audience asked that he do a few. With a warm smile Tariri, pleased at the request, quickly complied by mimicking the song of five birds.

After a few days in the metropolis it was obvious that his heart was in his jungle home. In spite of all the beautiful things in Lima, he did not want to stay because his tribe needed him. He was also anxious about the sick son whom he had left at Yarinacocha.

At his final meeting with President Odría, he expressed a desire to aid in the civilization of his tribal area. He also offered to clear and prepare a landing strip for airplanes "because I saw that the Chief's [president's] eyes were good." In turn, the president gave him a gift of one hundred and fifty machetes for his men, as well as thread for the women.

In taking leave of the president, he said, "I could not go without bidding good-by to such a high Chief as you."

Always ready with an eloquent speech appropriate for the occasion, Tariri went from news conference to presidential palace to school gathering with grace and a sense of mission. In addressing a group of students, he said, "I feel that every man is my brother, every woman my sister, and every child my son." He urged the students, "Do not leave the path planned by God."

In recalling the fantastic visit to the outer Peruvian space of Lima, Tariri recounted how he was subjected to an encephalogram by a curious scientist:

At some chief's place they wanted to look inside my head with a machine. They put little pieces of metal here and there all over my head. I thought, They probably think I am lying and want to see if I am a great chief.

When they had put those things all over my head and also on my heart, I was worried. I was sad. I thought, Maybe they want to kill me with this machine. Then I said to myself, No, I will be very strong.

So the machine went *zing! zing!* and it kept throwing out my words and throwing out my words, and it kept throwing out paper. "Let us find out about Tariri," they were probably saying.

But I was greater than the machine. So they said, "He has a big heart. He knows many things. He is telling the truth."

Then they opened the machine, took off the pieces of metal, and let me go.

Tariri returned to Base Yarinacocha on his way home to the Pushaga River. In expressing appreciation for the medical and spiritual help of the Wycliffe family at the Base, he said in his farewell speech:

I am going soon. I am leaving you happily because you all know God. But the people where I live do not know God. I am sad because they do not know God's Word. I want to tell them all of His Word. Then they will probably come to know God. I am even going to tell the women of God's Word. The women here are like my sisters. I want my home to be like that. I want the upriver people to know God, too. When they have all come to know God's Word and have left the strong *masato*, then we will live happily. Now all of you help me. The devil might want to stop me. Then how will the people come to know God? Everyone will look at my life. Pray for me. I will pray for you.

Upon arriving in the tribe, he called his people together to report on his trip. The group gathered at sundown, and the discourse continued through the night. He repeatedly mentioned the fact that God took him to Lima to tell the "chiefs" there what God had done for a jungle chief.

Beth Hinson wrote of his return:

"We were afraid he would be spoiled by all the attention he had received. However, he returned with only a strong desire that all his tribe be saved. One day he called the people together to receive the machetes and thread the president had sent. Before he gave them out, he explained the way of salvation. That afternoon the witchdoctor and one of our schoolboys accepted the Lord."

Tariri distributed half of the machetes to his people. He then went to visit a neighboring chief with whom he had been warring and made him a gift of the rest.

XIII

I Went to the Country of the Kirinko

In June, *1957*, Tariri was invited to participate in the Ralph Edwards "This Is Your Life" telecast in Hollywood, California, honoring Rachel Saint. She was accompanied by Dayuma, the Auca woman whom she had met at a jungle hacienda in Ecuador. Dayuma had fled from her tribe after her father had been cruelly speared and buried alive.

Tariri's wife Irina and their youngest child flew with him to the United States. As a memento of the occasion Ralph Edwards gave Tariri a portable radio, a luxury he had longed for.

From the West Coast Tariri went to visit on the East Coast. He was taken to call upon the Peruvian ambassador to the United States in Washington, D.C. Fifteen Peruvians were in the ambassador's office when Tariri gave his full story, with his customary animation. They had known of the Shapra tribe as a problem area and were amazed to learn that the eloquent speaker, standing a few feet from them, was a chief of the tribe. The ambassador clearly explained that Tariri was a product of a Bible-translating mission.

A problem in diplomacy arose when the ambassador wanted to present Tariri with a box of cigars. "In my tribe, only the witchdoctor smokes," said Tariri.

In reporting the visit, Tariri said later:

I went to see the ambassador of my country in Washington. I liked him so much that I gave him my gold and green beetle earrings. I wanted him to tell people when he shows them, "These were given to me by a man who before killed many, but now believes in Jesus."

In New York a reporter interviewed Tariri for an hour, focusing her interrogation upon his reaction to things in the United States. He told her frankly that he had come for one reason: to tell what Jesus had done for him. The reporter had been chain-smoking throughout the interview, and displayed some impatience with Tariri's insistence on talking about Jesus. The reporter then asked if he objected to her smoking. Tariri commented, as he had to the ambassador, that in his land only the witchdoctor smoked.

In New York Tariri attended a meeting of the Billy Graham Crusade. The New York Herald-Tribune *for June 16, 1957, carried the following report:*

"A befeathered jungle chief who used to hunt heads in the wilds of Peru listened to Billy Graham preach, then nodded his head vigorously. 'Great teacher,' he said in his deep basso. 'Much authority.'

"Chief Tariri, head of the Shapra tribe in the north-central Peruvian jungles west of the Andes, was among 16,000 listeners to Graham last night at Madison Square Garden.

" 'I wish my tribe could see it,' he said in his native Candoshi tongue, referring to the hundreds who streamed down the aisle at the end of the service to 'accept Christ.'

"The chief, his words translated by missionary Lorrie Anderson, of Ramsey, N. J., added, 'I wish everyone would receive the Lord.' That's what he did four years ago, and ordered his tribe to quit head-hunting.

"But he said he still has occasional trouble in preventing killings, particularly when someone wants to carry out a

*death of revenge in conformity with ancient tribal tradi-
tions.*

*" 'God,' he added, the beads shaking about his neck as he
gestured, 'loves everyone.'*

*"The chief was brought here by a television program, and
because his tribe had been praying for Graham's New York
Crusade, he wanted to take in the services himself, to report
back how it was doing.*

*" 'Many warriors learning God's Word here,' he said.
'Women, too. But they talk too much.' Miss Anderson duly
interpreted it."*

*A local newspaper in New Jersey gave considerable space
to reporting the impact which Tariri made upon Lorrie
Anderson's home town:*

FORMER HEADHUNTER TELLS RIDGEWOOD ABOUT CHRIST
*Peruvian Jungle Chief Preaches the Gospel in Native
Tongue in Village Store.*

*"A former Peruvian jungle headhunter preached the gospel
in his native tongue yesterday in a Ridgewood store while
scores of persons listened.*

*"Tariri's impression of this country was mixed. He was
constantly amazed at the mechanical civilization he saw here.
The chief was delighted by a water sprinkler on a lawn that
he controlled by turning the power on and off. He felt a deep
loss when a Ridgewood patrolman's whistle that was given to
him was lost. A smile covered his olive brown face when the
whistle was found.*

*"Among some of the things he would like to take home with
him are: electric light switches to turn on lights, a suitcase, a
model of a 4-engine plane, a watermelon, some cherries, and
two very large dogs. Tariri has seven children back in his
jungle home."*

Upon his return to Peru, Tariri recounted his trip as fol-
lows:

Irina said to me when we were going to the country of the
kirinko, "You know, there are a lot of bad diseases there. We will
surely die." I was also a little worried, but I said, "No, I do not
think so."

I was sad as we went. Suppose my child dies? I thought. And
will we really return? What will happen?

My wife was very sad in the airplane. I squeezed her hand so
much that mine hurt. She was trembling with fear. I was talking to
God for her when we were so high up there. My head ached most
of the time.

Then along the way I was thinking, Why am I sad? So I talked
with God and said, Help me. As I was worrying and thinking,
Maybe the plane will crash, or, Maybe I will get sick and die, I
began to talk to God. I said to Him, Give me peace. Why did you
send me here? I will tell your Word very much here. Help me tell
your Word well. Help me to say the words well. Make my mouth
light. Give me your words, put them within me.

And so I went to the country of the *kirinko.*

But I did not expect to see Tiyotari. There we were talking and
making a lot of noise and then Tiyotari, the one who had been to
our country, came out! This was in the chief's house [the Ralph
Edwards studio]. My eyes were startled! It was just as if it were in
a dream. I wiped my eyes out and I thought, Am I dreaming?
Maybe it is in death. What is Tiyotari doing away up here? "Is it
you, sister?" I said. "How many years ago did I see you on the
Pushaga? But I have not forgotten you. I have kept thinking about
you very much. I did not know where you were."

And there far away we saw Dayuma. She came running out, too.
I had been told about her in Peru. I was happy to see her with
Tiyotari.

In the chief's house there were many lights. My wife Irina was
afraid. Many lights hung over our heads.

In all the places where we visited there were many, many colored lights. I would like to have many lights in my house so that my people could enjoy seeing them.

I talked to everyone as my brother and told how I used to live. "Let your ears listen to me," I said. "Let us all live well. Let us love Jesus only. Let us follow Him."

We went here and there day and night. I was not ashamed nor did I think bad things in my heart. I just happily told God's Word.

We saw that there were many things to eat, but we stayed hungry because they were strange to us. In order to get my wife to eat something I would tell her, "This is very good. Eat it." She would answer me, "All right," and she would eat a little. Then she would feel like throwing it up and I would tell her, "Do not do it. That would cause us shame." Then I would pass her some food, saying, "This is *pawiana*," or some other of the foods we know, and she would feel better.

The cars bothered me. My wife told me that in time I would enjoy it, but it is not true. My wife enjoyed it.

At first we could not sleep at night.

They took us to a big store where there were many toys for the children, and we bought some for ours. Then my wife was happy.

The Peruvians are my countrymen. We live in the same country. We live together. The *kirinko* live in another place. How can I place it? Perhaps they live downriver, and we, upriver. Their country is pretty, but I like Peru better. I prefer the woods. But now that I do not fight, my tribe needs the help of the chiefs of our country.

I pray a lot, too, for the one [Ralph Edwards] who gave me the radio. We love to listen to it. I gave him some of my *moropshi* ornaments even though there are not any where I live now. We pay a lot for them.

In one place [San Francisco] I saw very big canoes [steamships]. I looked and looked at them. How I would like to have one on the Pushaga River for our tribe to use!

There are many people in that land. In one meeting in New

York I saw more people than I thought there were in all the world. The world is very large. Before, I thought that Iquitos was the end of the world. I had never gone to Iquitos, but I had heard about it.

The *kirinko* probably wondered why I came, just as I used to wonder why Mpawachi and Monchanki came to our country. I hope they know that I wanted to love them like brothers.

XIV

How My Son Was Healed

In 1963 Tariri's son Tsirimpo, crippled in both feet from birth, was taken to the Mayo Clinic in Rochester, Minnesota, for a successful operation. Wycliffe nurse Amy Rude, who accompanied him on the long trip, reported:

"In the operating room before his surgery Tsirimpo told those present (through an interpreter) that he wanted his feet to get well because 'I want to teach God's Word when I go back, on rivers where the Word has not yet been taken.' Tsirimpo left an impressive testimony at the Rochester hospital.

" 'Cases like this make life worth while,' said his surgeon."

My son Tsirimpo, being crippled, we took to the doctor at Yarinacocha. I said to my brother the doctor, "What can we do?" The doctor said, "If you send him to our country, they probably can fix him." And then my heart was happy. "That is what we will do," I said. "That will probably make him better. If God helps them and my child is made better, I will be happy. My poor son suffers this way."

After I had said that, and when they said, "All right, we will send him," my heart was very sad. He will die, I thought. How will it be? What if he dies when they cut? But my son said, "Father, pray for me. Do not stop praying." When he said that, I thought in my heart, God will help him. Did God not take the man's rib long ago and make a woman out of it, out of his own rib? If God was able to do that long ago, why should Tsirimpo die now? God will help him.

Then I thought, What if the devil is very strong? No. God alone is very strong.

My son went to the *kirinko* country. Then for awhile I did not hear about him. How is my child? I wondered. I said to God, *You* are looking after him. Take care of my son. For you have said, "Even when a person goes far away, I am with him. Even though you are lost, I am there." Did you not say that? Thinking that, I prayed a lot.

So the doctor cut on my son and he made him better. They slapped something like clay all over his legs [casts]. When I heard that, I was sad. "Poor boy," I said, "he had to be all by himself and suffer." That is why I cried a little. Even though he was still alive, I cried for him because he suffered.

Then I thought, Now I am so happy because my son wants to come home. My heart is happy.

My brother the doctor fixed him up. God helped him. A doctor cannot raise people up by himself. It is God who gives the order. He tells the doctor to work, and the doctor works, and God then heals. The doctor says, with his eyes shining, "I made him better." But it was God who gave the order and helped him.

If my son had not known God, what would he have done? The doctor might have been unable to help him. He would not have been able to walk so soon. But God put His healing hand on him and said, "Let it be healed."

God gave the medicines. He caused the plants to grow and people learned how to make the medicines from them. Sewing the skin and placing the medicine only help to heal. God makes the skin grow back. He helps in every way, He helps the doctor. If God does not help the doctor, it is possible for him to kill a person.

Now that my son is able to walk and he is back at Yarinacocha, as Monchanki told me, I am happy.

I talk much with God who healed him. Thank you, Father, I say. How many times did you heal my child! You are great!

My son has come back home. I am happy, very happy. Saying that, I live.

XV

We Want to See God's Word on Paper

Whoever has God's Word is very happy. We do well if we have God's Word on paper. For then we can always learn and tell about Him.

You should truly love God, you who do have God's Word in your language. Why is it that having God's Word you do not believe it? It is a happy person who can learn letters and look at God's Word.

God's Word is good. It is the one and only thing that is truly good.

God's Word is never mixed up. The message gets through straight. God shoots through with His Spirit like sun's rays to those who love Him. Thus it is impossible to miss when we talk with God.

God also goes with us everywhere. It is impossible to hide from Him, even in a cave. If you should go into the ground, or underwater, God is also there. Thus it is impossible for His message to get confused. It is impossible for it to be blocked, since God is very powerful.

We people just do not compare with God. God's Spirit comes down here to us. Does God's Word not say that His Spirit came down here, directing Himself only upon those who were following Him? He came to all upon the earth who loved God and directed their thoughts by His Word. God's Word gives peace. It helps one to forget bad things done to hurt one.

I am very sad when I hear that there are those who want to make war, and kill. Why is it? Are they as we were when we had not heard God's Word?

If it were not that they do not know my language, I would write a letter and send it to them. But I do not know their language. I would say, What are you thinking? Did you, and not God, create the heavens? Who placed the heavens and the sun? Who put the moon in its place? Who made the earth? Who made food for you to eat? Should God take away your food, bread and all, then what would you eat? You would die of hunger. If God should take back all the animals, He would punish all your children with hunger and death.

Since it was God who put everything in the earth in order for us to live strong, He can also send a large flood to punish those who do not love His Word. It is only right that He punish.

Would one live happily should all the earth be covered with a flood or everything burned up with fire? God will burn the earth with flaming fire when Jesus returns.

The one who does not love, even though he claims to know God, does not live right. The devil holds him back, and throws up a cloud of dust again and again to mix up his thinking. When people are like that, it is easy for them to deceive and lie. They are unable to speak the whole truth.

Where have you seen in God's Word that you should desire bad things? What have you learned out of God's Word? Who ordered you to be bad? Who put these bad thoughts in your mind? You were given a mind to use. You cannot think by yourself. Should He take away your mind, you would be senseless. You would be like animals, like the woolly monkeys, or more like turtles, having turtles' brains. A turtle's mind cannot think. When it sees one of us, it just keeps on eating and is not one bit afraid. That is the way you would be, just senseless like a turtle. God gave us people minds to rule the earth. So think about that. Stop thinking bad things.

God never said to fight. He said, "Make my Word known to all. Teach my whole Word to people everywhere." Why do you not obey?

You have imagined this bad thing by yourself, because you do not obey God. You stumble easily and fall over a log. God's feet are firm. It is impossible for Him to fall.

God says that we must always tell His Word to all. Many people do not believe God's Word as I do today. They do not care. How can they be like that when Jesus was killed but went up to heaven again? Having gone up a hill, he went up into the clouds. All the people on the hill looked. He had been covered by a heavy cloud. As they looked and said, "Where has Jesus gone?" some angels came. God had sent them. They said, "What are you looking for Jesus for? As you have seen Him go, just like that He will come again." Jesus exists now because He went up. He went up in His body.

Where is He? Could one's eye make Him out? No. One's eye is not enough to know Him. Even so, He exists! He is alive! He is coming in His very own body, and those who love Him will see Him again. But those who do bad will all be punished. Not a single person can escape. Where can one take cover? You cannot hide in a hole, so where will you hide? Then what? I say, This you must believe!

You suppose you will be the most powerful. Do you think you are wise? No. God is much wiser than we are. We are just fooling ourselves, thinking this way. Our mouths speak great things, but our talk just does not compare with God. God alone is the greatest. That is what I think about seeking power.

Those who do not love Jesus will live with the devil in darkness. That place is no good. It is impossible to be happy there. They will be lost.

This is what God's Word teaches. We want to see it. We want to look at it often.

XVI

We Teach Our Enemies God's Word

In 1959 Bible translators John and Sheila Tuggy went to Tariri's tribe to help in the expanding work, including Bible translation, literacy, and the training of indigenous church leaders. Several Candoshi areas were asking for bilingual schools, but tribal teachers needed to be prepared to instruct first in their Indian tongue, then in Spanish. The Swiss Indian Mission Bible School, located near Base Yarinacocha and co-operating with Wycliffe, was assisting in the preparation of Christian teachers and pastors.

In 1962 a peaceful contact was made with the upriver enemy Candoshi in order to give them the Gospel. Yampisa (Pincho's nephew and grandson of Old Shotka), who lived with Tariri's group, made a visit, taking with him a record player and Gospel records in the Candoshi language. Yampisa had been studying at the Bilingual School at Yarinacocha and at the nearby Bible School. He was well received by his upriver relatives. He was flown to the mouth of the Siquanga River in a Wycliffe float plane.

In 1963 John and Sheila Tuggy made a trip to the upriver Candoshi. They were also cordially received.

Tariri tells of events leading up to Yampisa's missionary journey upriver:

I will tell you about the time eight years ago when my upriver enemy was killing me. He caused me to suffer much. He was waiting for an opportunity to face me directly. On the first shot he missed me, then he shot again, but God saved me.

Those were my upriver relatives from the Siquanga River that came. God had said not to hate people, even though they are like that. He said, "Love your enemy, even though he wants to kill you." But I hated them because they had shot me. I said I would never speak to them again, since they killed several of our people also. It is an unheard of thing to make up with that kind of enemy.

Thus I thought, until I realized that God did not want me to be like that. He wants me to speak with them and to love everyone.

Now I am sending Shimpotka and Yampisa to deliver my messages to them. Thus I hope to be able to speak face to face again someday. Since God says not to hate, I do not now hate.

Yampisa, upon his return, gave a vivid account of his trip:

I am going to tell you a little bit about when I went to teach God's Word. After I attended Bible School I went back to my country to teach my relatives. I was worried that my mother would not go with me because she had been unwilling to go upriver. We prayed about it and God made her willing to go, and I went happily upriver with my mother.

We went in the airplane and we landed at the mouth of the Siquanga River where the upriver people live. I was sad because I wondered if any of my relatives would come to get us right away since they lived so far upriver. We sat on the beach and waited for them. Then on the afternoon of the same day, they came. They had been hunting only three hours away. My heart was very happy, for God had helped us.

We went along in the canoe. Since it was late, we made camp at dusk, and I taught them God's Word. Among others, one of my brothers-in-law came. After I had taught them a little that night, we slept. The next day we continued upriver and slept out another night. We camped at the shelters which they had made to sleep in while they are hunting. So I taught my relatives God's Word again that night. We were having to camp along the way because they lived far upstream. We did not arrive at their houses for three days.

One night after I had taught, one named Mashingashi said to me, "I would like to receive God's Word soon. I would like to receive right away." And he listened happily to all I taught him and he wanted to receive Jesus right away. I thought in my heart, He is surely telling the truth. Even though I have not taught him a lot, yet he wants God's Word. And he received Jesus along the way and we continued on. Finally we got to the place where they lived.

I taught them God's Word there also. When I got there, my uncles and other relatives were worried because there was no house for me to stay in. They said, "Where are you going to teach us God's Word?" I said, "If we all work together, we can build a house quickly." So they did build a house with great joy. They all came and we worked together and finished building the house quickly. When we had finished, that is where I stayed. They wanted to build me a great big house, but I said, "I am not going to be here very long, only about a month. Just build me a shelter."

And so we gathered together every day and I taught them God's Word. My uncles and other relatives happily listened to God's Word. When we arrived there with Mashingashi who had received Jesus, people began to want Jesus and to want to follow God. That is why everyone said they wanted to follow Jesus also. Beginning then, some others received Jesus also.

We gathered together every morning and continued until noon. Many had come to hear the Word and I would tell them it was time to rest, but some of my uncles did not want to rest. Because they happily gathered together, my heart was happy. I saw that they really wanted to know God's Word, then at sundown we would stop again.

I would say, "Why go hungry? Go and eat and we will gather again." And as we were busy gathering together day after day for

God's Word, we ran out of food. They said, "What shall we do?" And we prayed and decided that we would go fishing with poison. All my uncles said to me, "If we go fishing tomorrow with poison and catch a lot of fish and smoke it and put it aside, then we can eat that day after day and we can gather together and hear God's Word without having to stop."

We fished with poison in a tiny lake and we got so many fish that my uncles were amazed. My uncles said to me, "How is it that we caught so many fish even in this small lake? Surely it must be that we prayed and asked God for it, and God said, 'So that they can continue to hear my Word, I will give this to them.' " And we fished, and though there were lots of people, everybody caught lots of fish.

When my uncles asked me about it, I said, "I will tell you a story about Jesus. Jesus' disciples had worked hard all night fishing, and they had not gotten anything. And so at dawn, as they had not caught any fish, and they were not thinking of anyone coming along, someone came along and said, 'Children, do you have any fish?' They said, 'No, we have not caught any.' So Jesus said, 'Throw your net on the right side of the boat,' and they did. They pulled out so many fish that they could not lift it." That is what I told my uncles, and they said, "Well, that is the way it is."

Then we ran out of food again. I said to my uncles, "We had better go hunting." But we did not get much. Then one man went and shot a deer. Even though they had never eaten deer before, the people ate it anyway because they wanted to hear God's Word every day.

The next day we were hungry again. We went out hunting, but all of the animals were very wild. We came back empty-handed. As some of the men came home and neared the clearing, they saw lots of animals. They said to me, "Surely this is because God is with us. We have never seen it like this before. But now since we are busy with God's Word, we see animals right close by."

Then my Uncle Toripi said to me, "What am I going to do about following God? I have killed many people. I have made many suffer."

I told my uncle that God was able to cleanse his heart, and that if he received Jesus, God would cleanse his heart from even this sin.

He said to me also, "I want to know God's Word and I want to receive Jesus, but I am like a witchdoctor. How can I get rid of this power within me? Maybe if you give me worm medicine and I take it and throw up, it will get rid of this power."

But I said to him, "No, that would never do it. How would medicine help you get rid of this power of the witchdoctor? However, receiving Jesus can do it. Your heart will be made new by God's power."

Then he said, "I did many bad things. I lived bad. I killed many people. For witchcraft I drank lots of *ayahuasca*." He was very sad.

"God will change you," I said.

After that he said, "I will receive Jesus now."

So I said, "Receive Him."

Other people received Jesus. Though it was very hard for them, they wanted Jesus right away, and then it seemed that they had known Him for a long time.

Toripi took his new drum which he had made for drinking parties and said, "What good is this? We are not going to drink any more." He broke it and put it in the fire and burned it. He said, "If I break this, I will not beat it and get drunk any more. If anyone else around here tries to make one for drinking parties, we will put him to shame. Some of the others said that they wanted to follow God too, and so I will remind them of that."

Then Tsowinki, who is very much of a witchdoctor and has been for a long time, came to my house and told me that he wanted to receive Jesus. "I want to follow Him," he said. He asked me many questions and I told him. He said, "What shall I do? After I receive Jesus and follow God, what shall I do after giving up witchdoctoring and drinking *ayahuasca*?

He thought about it a lot. Then he said, "I want to leave *ayahuasca*. I suffer drinking it all the time. I get drunk from it and chant and people keep coming to me and ask me to heal their sick ones. So I will receive Jesus. Then when people say to me, 'Heal him,' I will say, 'Since I have received Jesus I do not practice witchcraft any more.' People will not bother me."

So I said, "That is right."

And he said, "I want God's Word, then I will live well. I want to leave *ayahuasca*."

When he had received Jesus he asked me, "Brother, what if someone is sick and they bring him to me and say, 'Practice witchcraft on him?' What shall I do? What shall I do if a person is dying?"

So I said to him, "You used the power of the devil before. When you trust God and you love Jesus, it is possible to heal by prayer."

So when I had said that, he thought about it silently and said, "That is good. That is what I will do."

Before he had received Jesus, I noticed that he had not taken the medicine for tuberculosis that Monchanki sent. There was a lot there and he had not taken it because he was a witchdoctor. Then as soon as he received Jesus, the next day in fact, he began to take the medicine. He said, "Why should I fast any more? I was afraid that the medicine would kill my magic darts, but now that Jesus has cleansed my heart, I am not worrying about that any more." So he began to take the medicine and was not afraid of it any more. When I saw that, I knew that he must be telling the truth, that he had really received Jesus.

Then all the people said, "Who is going to come and teach us to look at the paper? We want a school, we want to learn. When we just hear God's Word we forget a lot of it, but if we had it written down and could look at it, then we would not forget it. Then we would really come to know it."

So I said to myself, Who will teach them here? And I said, "God knows. I really do not know who it will be. There really is nobody right now. I could do it but it would not be easy. I have two years more in Bible School and I want to finish that first. I have not learned a lot yet and I want to learn more before I teach."

When my uncles heard that, they were very sad. But I said, "I will come back."

Then they said, "We will be dead by then, waiting for you to come back."

So I told them, "You will not die if God takes care of you. God will look after you, even though you have no teacher here to help you."

And they said that they would trust in God.

I want to ask my friends to pray for me as I study, that I will finish. I want very much to teach God's Word and work hard doing it.

Also because you prayed, I learned of God. Even though it was far away, Monchanki arrived at our country. So I am happy because you helped us and some of us have come to know God. Now if God helps us, we will be able to teach our own people. I want to work hard with my people to tell them God's Word.

That is all I will say. Pray for the people at Siquanga that all those who received Jesus will keep following Him.

As Tariri has learned of the need for Bible translation in many other tribes, his missionary zeal has grown. He constantly expresses appreciation for those who brought him the Word, and urges more translators to go to other tribes:

God has asked us to go to all lands where there are people who have not heard God's Word. If we really love God's Word, we should take it and send it wherever people have not heard.

God has filled the earth with people speaking different languages. Since they live in hatred we must take His Word to all places and to all people.

When we have taken God's Word to the last places, Jesus will return. When Jesus returns, God will punish all those who do away with His Word. There will be no place to hide, even though one might be the greatest of chiefs. Should one try to make a strong and large hiding place to live in, even that would not stop God. But those that love God, He will take up. It will be wonderful when that happens.

Take God's Word everywhere, showing that you love Him!

When Jesus comes here again, He will make a nice world for those that love Him. Right now we live on a bad earth and our hearts are sick with bad things which God cannot look on. Let us tell His Word to all people.

Just think! God made man so easily from a lump of dirt. Then He sent men far away, here and there all over the world. He also sent animals everywhere to feed the Piros, the Shipibos, the Amueshas, and all the other tribes. He made all people. We are all of the same flesh. He did not make anyone different. We all have blood, flesh, and a heart. Why should we hate each other?

Look. Now I have many brothers. All the Peruvians and *kirinko* that love God have been made my brothers because we have the same blood, the blood of Jesus.

If all chiefs would start sending people out with God's Word, then Jesus would be happy and He would return.

Look at my brother [Townsend]. Look how God has helped him as he sends out people to take God's Word. God has him for a real chief who does not do away with God's Word. God is probably well pleased when we obey Him.

When Jesus comes again, all those who love Him will come together. They will talk together, saying, "Thus and thus has God done to me." God will not forget who it was who took His Word to all people.

This is what we want to do now: We want to send many people to those who were our enemies. We will teach them about God, as He has asked us to do.

Soon I will go to the Muratos. I will be teaching them God's Word right where I made war before. I have many relatives there.

God will no longer turn His back on us, but He will face us, since He has forgiven us. God will help us much. He has given us His Spirit, joy, peace, and life without worry.

I would like to talk with anyone who can come to tell the people upriver about God. If you ever want to talk this over with me, come and see me.

My name is Tariri. Come, let us talk together about God and His Word.

Glossary

achiote (ah-chee-*oh*-te)   red seed from a jungle bush used for face-painting and for magic purposes

Achual (ah-choo-*wahl*)   Jivaro tribe adjacent to the Shapras, a small group of whom are friendly to Tariri's group

Aguaruna (ah-gwah-*roo*-nah)   Jivaro tribe adjacent to the Shapras and partly friendly to them

ají (ah-*hee*)   Spanish word, derived from Quechua, for hot chili peppers

Apanchi (ah-*pahn*-chee)   Candoshi name for God

Arosa (ah-*roe*-sah)   wife of Old Chiriapa, Tariri's brother-in-law; daughter of Old Shotka

arotama (ah-*roe*-tah-mah)   Candoshi word for power of long life

Arturo (ahr-*too*-roe)   Peruvian *patrón* friendly to Tariri

Auca (*ah*-oo-cah)   A once fierce tribe of Ecuador which killed five missionaries in 1956 (see *Through Gates of Splendor* by Elisabeth Elliot, Harper & Row, 1957), but for whom Rachel Saint of the Wycliffe Bible Translators is now translating the Bible (see *The Dayuma Story* by Ethel Emily Wallis, Harper & Row, 1960).

ayahuasca (ah-yah-*wahs*-cah)   narcotic obtained from a jungle plant

barbasco (bar-*bahs*-coe)   poison from a jungle root used for fishing

Candoshi (cahn-*doe*-shee)   tribe in northern Peru to which the Sharpra group belongs

Cangasa (cahn-*gah*-sah)   river in northern Peru near the Andes

canishi (cah-*nee*-shee)   Candoshi word for evil spirit; name of a bird said to have supernatural powers

chacra (*chah*-crah)   Spanish word for a cultivated plot of land

Chapuri (chah-*poo*-ree)   river near which Nochumata, Tariri's father, lived

Chuinta (choo-*een*-tah)   river which runs into Lake Rimachi where Tariri's father once lived

Chumpi (*choom*-pee)   friend of Tariri's father who learned the art of head-shrinking from the Achuales

cocona (coe-*coe*-nah)   acid jungle fruit

Huambisa (wham-*bee*-sah)   Jivaro tribe adjacent to the Shapras

Iquitos (ee-*kee*-tohs)   large city in inland Peru

Irina (ee-*ree*-nah)   Tariri's second wife

JAARS   Jungle Aviation and Radio Service, a subsidiary of Wycliffe Bible Translators

Kamposoro (cham-poe-*soe*-roe)   young Achual who lived with upriver Shapras of the enemy group

Kasimoro (cah-see-*moe*-roe)   Tariri's uncle who taught him to kill and take heads

kontoma (cone-*doe*-mah)   a palm, fruit of which is used in Shapra ritual; the heart of the tree is a delicacy

koraka (coo-*rah*-cah)   Quechua word for chief

Korima (koh-*ree*-mah)   Shapra ancestor, expert in the art of making blowguns

Maama (*mah*-ah-mah)   Shapra ancestor remembered for his teachings of tribal lore

Makiya (*mah*-kee-yah)   river on which the Achuales lived

Manchonka (mahn-*chone*-kah)   small river in northern Peru where the Shapra ancestors lived

Marañon (*mah*-rah-nyon)   large river in northern Peru

Marasho (*mah*-rah-show)   Tariri's first wife, mother of Tsirimpo

masato (mah-*sah*-toe) Spanish word for drink made from masticated yuca

Mashingashi (mah-sheeng-*gah*-shee)   upriver Shapra who accepted Christ during Yampisa's missionary journey

Matarina (mah-tah-*ree*-nah)   Tariri's little daughter

Mawuia (mah-*wee*-ah)   river on which Achuales lived

Mbisa (*mbee*-sah)   friend of Tariri's Uncle Kasimoro

metori (*me*-toe-ree)   bird of ill omen to the Candoshi

Mikaya (mee-*kah*-yah)   Old Tsowinki's wife, sister of Shimpotka

Monchanki (mone-*chahng*-kee)   Lorrie Doris Anderson, named for Tariri's deceased sister

Morona (moe-*roe*-nah)   large river in northern Peru near Tariri's territory moropshi (moe-*rope*-shee) Candoshi word for certain large seed ornaments greatly valued by them

mota (*moe*-tah) an edible root; also used in Candoshi magic rites

Mpawachi (mpah-*wah*-chee) Candoshi name given to Doris Cox

Mpona (*mpoe*-nah) ancestor whose teaching Tariri followed

Murato (moo-*rah*-toe) Spanish name for tribal group of Candoshi

Nochumata (*noe*-choo-mah-tah) Tariri's father

Old Chiriapa (chee-ree-*ah*-pah) Tariri's brother-in-law killed by upriver Shapras

Old Shotka (*shote*-kah) upriver Shapra chief

Old Tsowinki (tsoe-*wing*-kee) upriver enemy, stepson of Old Shotka

Pastaza (pahs-*tah*-sah) large river in Ecuador and in northern Peru

patrón (pah-*trone*) Spanish word for boss or employer

pawiana (paw-*eah*-nah) food of the Shapras

Pincho (*peen*-choe) upriver Shapra, teenage son of Old Shotka

piripiri (pee-*ree*-pee-*ree*) plant, root of which is supposed to have magic powers

Pirocha (pee-*roe*-chah) upriver Shapra, son of Old Shotka who came to kill Tariri

Pucucura (poo-koo-*koo*-rah) stream which flows into the Morona River

Pushaga (poo-*shah*-gah) tributary of the Morona on which Tariri lived when the missionaries first arrived

Rimachi (ree-*mah*-chee) largest lake of the Peruvian jungle near which Tariri's ancestors lived

Shapra (*shah*-prah) part of the Candoshi tribe of which Tariri is chief

Shimpotka (sheem-*pote*-kah) nephew of Old Shotka who has lived most of his life with Tariri's group

Shiniki (shee-*nee*-kee) Tariri's brother-in-law

shoroshoro (shoh-roh-*shoh*-roh) Candoshi name for a jungle bird with a long, low tail

Siquanga (see-*kwahng*-gah) tributary of the Morona River upriver from Tariri's group

Tamshiyaco   (tahm-shee-*yah*-coe)   tributary of the Pushaga where Shimpotka lived

Tanchima   (tahn-*chee*-mah)   one of Tariri's group

Tariri   (tah-*ree*-ree)   ancestor for whom Chief Tariri was named

Tiyotari   (tee-*yoe*-tah-ree)   Tariri's Candoshi name for Rachel Saint

Toripi   (toe-*ree*-pee)   upriver Shapra converted through the teaching of his nephew Yampisa

Totarika   (toe-tah-*ree*-kah)   Tariri's grandfather; also name of Tariri's son who died when he was nine years old

toucan   (*too*-cahn)   jungle bird with long yellow bill, black feathers on the body, and red and yellow tail feathers

Tsirimpo   (tsee-*reem*-poe)   witchdoctor killed by Tariri's father; also name of Tariri's son by his first wife, Marasho

Tsowinki   (tsoe-*wing*-kee)   Tariri's half-brother, married to the sister of Old Shotka

Tspako   (*tspah*-koe)   Tariri's paternal grandmother

Victorino   (veek-toe-*ree*-noe)   friendly rubber trader who introduced the missionaries to Tariri

Wanka   (*wahng*-kah)   Huambisa chief, friend of Tariri

Warispa   (wah-*rees*-pah)   Tariri's uncle, a witchdoctor

wiracocha   (wee-rah-*koe*-chah)   Candoshi word, from the Quechua, for foreigner

Yampisa   (yahm-*pee*-sah)   grandson of Old Shotka who went upriver to evangelize his relatives

Yarinacocha   (yah-ree-nah-*coe*-chah)   Wycliffe's jungle base in Peru

Yonkantari   (yong-*kahn*-tah-ree)   river from which the Shapra ancestors came

Young Chiriapa   (chee-ree-*ah*-pah)   teenage upriver fellow married to Old Shotka's daughter

Young Shimpotka   (sheem-*pote*-kah)   half-brother of Yampisa

Young Shiniki   (shee-*nee*-kee)   Tariri's half-brother, a bilingual Shapra schoolteacher

yuca   (*yoo*-cah)   root of manioc, a large tuber, basic food of the Candoshi

Format by Mort Perry
Set in Linotype Janson
Composed, printed and bound by The Haddon Craftsmen, Inc.
HARPER & ROW, PUBLISHERS, INCORPORATED